SYMBOLS

• THAT SURROUND US •

Faithful Reflections

JOHAN VAN PARYS

Liguori
LIGUORI, MISSOURI

Imprimi Potest:
Harry Grile, CSsR, Provincial
Denver Province, The Redemptorists

Published by Liguori Publications
Liguori, Missouri 63057

To order, call 800-325-9521, or visit liguori.org.

Library of Congress Cataloging-in-Publication Data

Van Parys, Johan.
 Symbols that surround us : faithful reflections / Johan van Parys.—1st ed.
 p. cm.
 ISBN 978-0-7648-2070-0
 1. Christian art and symbolism. 2. Catholic Church—Liturgy. I. Title.
 BX1970.V318 2011
 246.088'282—dc23
 2011041988

Photos of Mass celebrants provided by the author and The Basilica of Saint Mary, Minneapolis

Liguori Publications, a nonprofit corporation, is an apostolate of the Redemptorists. To learn more about the Redemptorists, visit Redemptorists.com.

Printed in the United States of America
16 15 14 13 12 / 5 4 3 2 1
First Edition

CONTENTS

We thank the following photographers for their generous contributions to this book:

Seán P. Cardinal O'Malley, 38 (top); **Shutterstock**, iv, 3, 4, 6, 7, 8, 12, 14, 16, 18, 21, 25, 27, 51 (top), 64, 67, 73, 74, 75, 76, 77 (top), 88 (top), 118, 120, 132 (bottom), 138, 140, 142; **Johan van Parys**, ix, 30, 32, 34, 38 (bottom), 39, 41, 44, 54, 56, 57 (right), 58 (top left and right), 62 (top right), 66, 72, 90, 91, 122, 123, 128, 130, 132 (top), 134, 135, 136, 139, 145, 146 (top); **M. Jensen Photography Inc.**, x, 10, 20, 46, 49, 50, 52 (bottom), 69, 71, 77 (bottom), 80, 85 (top), 86, 87, 92 (bottom), 96, 99, 100, 101, 108, 109, 114, 117, 119, 125; **Denise Anderson**, 17, 33, 35, 40, 43, 51 (bottom), 52 (top), 58 (bottom), 59, 62 (top left), 78, 83, 84, 88 (bottom), 105, 107, 126, 141, 143, 144, 146 (bottom); **Daniel Miller**, 19, 24, 68; **Robert D. Habiger**, 22; **Gene Plaisted**, OSC, 23; **Dianne Towalski** of *The Catholic Spirit*, 28, 60 (top), 93; **John Korom** (courtesy of HGA Architects and Engineers), 36; **Mark Scheyer** (courtesy of Jackson & Ryan Architects), 37; **Gregory L. Tracy**, 42; **Chesley LLC**, 48 (copyright 1992); **M.J. Anderson**, 57 (left); **Helen McLean**, 60 (bottom); **Father David Darin**, 61; **Wikipedia**, 62 (bottom), 92 (top), 103; **Christopher Stroh**, 82; **Patrick E. O'Connor**, 85 (bottom); **Dave Hrbacek** of *The Catholic Spirit*, 111; **Christopher S. Pineo**, 121; **iStock**, 102, 131; **Timothy Backous**, OSB, 148

FOREWORD

Our lives are filled with symbols and symbolic acts, from the sign of the cross made on our forehead before we were baptized, to the pall placed on our coffin at the end of our lives. In addition, between these two milestones in our lives as Christians, symbols surround us.

Some symbols are obvious and easily understood, such as the crucifix many of us have in our homes. Others are more obscure and not as common, such as the moon under Mary's feet, or the eagle at the side of Saint John the Evangelist. Some symbols tell the story of the saints, others tell the story of our faith, while still others are an essential part of the liturgy and sacramental life of the Church. The latter are notable because the liturgy uses simple elements of our daily lives and turns them into life-altering worship symbols.

Symbols are so important in our daily and liturgical lives, it is important to make sure we are familiar with them. To that end, Johan van Parys offers an excellent introduction to some of the most significant symbols in our lives.

The aim of *Symbols That Surround Us: Faithful Reflections* is twofold. The book offers insight into our daily use of symbols and the symbolic acts that uniquely equip humans for the use of symbols in a religious context, as well as how our experience with such simple elements as water, fire, bread, and wine prepare us for their sacramental use.

Dr. van Parys then talks about our daily use of symbols and our experience with sacramental symbols on a human level, as in the primary sacramental symbols of baptismal waters, the Easter fire, and eucharistic bread and wine, as well as secondary symbols, such as a *Gospel Book*, a crucifix, or an altar table. Throughout, he offers opportunities to reflect on the meaning of these symbols and make further connections with our experiences of them.

The religious symbols discussed here are but a few of the many that surround us, but the groundwork the book lays encourages all of us to become more aware of and appreciate symbols on a deeper level. This understanding allows their impact to be even greater each time we encounter them in our lives of faith.

GIOVANNI CARDINAL LAJOLO
PRESIDENT EMERITUS OF THE
GOVERNORSHIP OF VATICAN CITY STATE

INTRODUCTION

Ever since I was a young boy, I have been enamored of my ninety-five-year-old great-aunt, who now lives in a retirement community in Belgium. She has always been beautiful and extremely captivating. Throughout her life, she enjoyed a successful career and has lived most of her adult life in a beautiful home in Brussels, the capital of Belgium.

After her husband died, she moved back to our small hometown to live in a retirement community. I went to visit her there not long after I learned she was suffering from dementia. As I knocked somewhat hesitantly and walked into her room, she nodded to invite me in. As we visited, she seemed physically well, and she talked about her life in a very animated way. I quickly realized, though, that she did not know who I was, which saddened me a great deal. As I got ready to leave, I asked if I could kiss her farewell. She agreed, and when I leaned in to kiss her cheeks, tears began streaming down her face. She looked at me and she said: "Johan, how sad that I did not recognize you. When will you come to see me again?" I cried with her, but by the time I left she had already forgotten who I was.

Although this may sound like a fairy tale, it was as if my kiss woke her up. Beyond our conversation and all the information I had provided her to prove that I was her grand-nephew, she only recognized me in what seemed a small gesture of my love. Yet for her, it had a profound impact.

My experience with my aunt is exactly how symbols work. That which appears simple or ordinary can hold great meaning. Symbols enable us to communicate on a deeper level when we do not have the words to do so. In a religious context, symbols enable us to express our faith in ways that would not be possible if we were to rely exclusively on words. Simple and unassuming water and bread in the right context have a great impact on those who encounter them. If a picture is worth a thousand words, then a symbol is surely worth a million.

Although we may not always be aware of them, symbols surround us, connect us to sacred images found in our churches, remind us of our faith, and support us in our private and public prayer as we celebrate the sacraments and engage in private devotions.

There are ten chapters in this book. The first chapter distinguishes between signs and symbols by looking at how symbols are essential to our sacraments. The second chapter reflects on our human experience and the fundamental symbols that are used for the liturgy: water, fire and light, oil, bread, and wine. The next two chapters look at the symbolic nature of the buildings in which we celebrate the liturgy and the symbolic contribution of the arts within them. The remaining chapters observe how liturgical furnishings, objects, vestments, and gestures function symbolically, and the concluding chapters consider the role of liturgical décor and sacred imagery. Each chapter concludes with a set of questions intended to encourage your own reflection on the many symbols we encounter in our daily lives.

May this journey through the rich world of symbols enrich your experience of the images that surround you to enhance your faith, your celebration of the liturgy, and all your encounters of prayer.

Statue of the Immaculate Conception covered with shell leis,
St. Benedict Catholic Church, Kailua-Kona, Hawaii

CHAPTER ONE

SIGNS, SYMBOLS, AND SACRAMENTS

I recently spoke with friends about how a bouquet of flowers can mean something very different to those who receive them. They can symbolize love and affection if shared between people who care for one another. However, if the affection is not mutual, the same flowers can be experienced as annoying or even considered a form of stalking. It is amazing that a simple bouquet of flowers can stir such strong feelings as love or fear so completely that an explanatory note is not needed. The flowers themselves communicate the message.

Though people most often communicate through spoken language, we enjoy many other ways to convey messages. Our body language, the way we dress, and established signs and

Easter Vigil, The Basilica of Saint Mary, Minneapolis

symbols—such as wedding rings, uniforms, and even hairstyles—inform others about who we are, what we do, and how we live. All these nonverbal exchanges are important in our daily lives and perhaps even more so when we express our faith and celebrate our liturgies. The sacraments, for example, consist of two essential elements that have come to be known as the *form* and the *matter* of a sacrament. The *form* is the verbal portion, or the words that are spoken during the celebration of the sacrament, such as when "I baptize you in the name of the Father, and of the Son and of the Holy Spirit" is declared in the celebration of baptism. The *matter* is the symbol that is used for the conferral of the sacrament, such as the water in the sacrament of baptism and the oil in the sacrament of confirmation. The words or *form* of the sacrament communicate rich theological truths that reveal the essence of the sacrament. Still, it is not until the words or *form* are united with the symbol or matter that the sacrament is realized. What would baptism be without water? Or Eucharist without bread or wine? Symbols are essential for the celebration of the sacraments.

This is why it is important to understand how our daily nonverbal communication forms an understanding for our use of symbols, as well as how signs and symbols are similar and yet different from one another. This foundation enables us to understand the symbols that enrich our liturgies more fully and thus engage in the celebration of the sacraments more deeply.

VERBAL VERSUS NONVERBAL LANGUAGE

Some years ago, I was presenting a lecture to a group of undergraduates at the University of Notre Dame. The topic was "Eucharistic Miracles," and I was well-prepared with images, music, and poetry. Yet none of the information about eucharistic miracles during the Middle Ages appeared to engage the students. They slouched in their chairs, yawned, showed little interest, and didn't take a single note. Afterward, one of the students congratulated me on the lecture, and although I heard his words, it was hard for me to believe him because of his slouching body language throughout my presentation. Though he said one thing, his posture communicated a much stronger message that was quite the opposite. This is but one example of the complexities of communication. Our message system is more than just words. Much of our communication occurs nonverbally and spills far beyond the linear sentences we share.

As with the students, our body language communicates great amounts of information. A smile can imply joy at an encounter. Our tears reveal sorrow. A wink may disarm an otherwise tense situation with its playfulness. There are also unfortunate and even unintended messages that body language can communicate, not unlike that of the students in my class. When we take this understanding of body language into the realm of worship, we might think about those who casually saunter up to receive holy Communion apparently distracted by everything around them. Though they may not realize the casual stance they express about receiving our Lord in the Eucharist, others may be scandalized by what appears to be disrespect.

A Sister of Charity

The way we dress is also a form of communication and reveals how we regard the event we are attending. When I was preparing to move to the United States, I was invited to the U.S. Embassy in Brussels for a seminar on appropriate behavior in U.S. society. One of the topics presented was on appropriate dress. The instructor suggested that people in the U.S. dress much more informally than Europeans. However, the instructor stressed there were different "levels" of informal dress. She explained that informal dress appropriate for a baseball game was not the same as what might be worn for a company barbecue, and that appropriate attire for the beach is different than what is worn for a run around the lake. Clothing indeed communicates much more than what the casual wearer might intend, even in the most informal of settings. This awareness of how clothing communicates becomes even clearer when we consider what is worn for more formal occasions. Most of us would not dream of wearing shorts, a rock concert T-shirt, and beach sandals to a funeral because it would not show the respect we would want to express to the deceased by more formal attire. In its most formal version, clothing can be highly symbolic, as at a wedding or during the celebration of any liturgy. If all the women guests wore long white gowns at a wedding ceremony, it would be quite confusing. Culture and custom dictate that only one woman wears white at a wedding, and that is the bride. And it is ritual garb that enables us to distinguish between deacons, priests, and bishops.

THE IMPORTANCE OF SIGNS AND SYMBOLS IN OUR DAILY LIVES

Most of us respond to daily messages communicated by signs and symbols, even if we do not notice it. We slow down and stop at a red light. We cross the street at a white-striped crosswalk. We give a heart-shaped box of chocolates on Valentine's Day. We exchange promise rings. We send flowers. We embrace. These are but a few of the many signs and symbols we might encounter in our lives. Signs and symbols communicate a lot in a little time, such as at a traffic light, or when words are not enough, as in the embrace received when someone close to us wants to offer comfort. In these situations, we rely on either signs or symbols to convey a fuller message than what is shared on the surface. Signs and symbols are closely related, yet they are different. What's the difference?

The word "sign" comes from the Latin word *signum*, meaning "mark." Essentially, signs are images that convey definite and communally agreed-upon information. Signs tell us to do or not to do something specific, such as to give right-of-way or drive no faster than thirty-five miles per hour.

Signs can only mean one thing. There can be no confusion about the meaning of a sign. When we see a red circular sign with a white bar in the middle, we know not to enter. There are different words on this sign all over the world, but its shape, red color, and white crossbar have acquired a meaning that communicates "do not enter," so we don't.

For the most part, a sign is chosen arbitrarily, and the connection between the sign and its meaning is random. There is neither a necessary nor even a natural connection between the meaning that it points at or signifies. A stop sign is octagonal or eight-sided for no particular reason. As a result, people have to learn how to read signs or understand their shape and color associations, such as with most traffic signs, before they can use them.

By contrast, symbols are not arbitrary and can communicate multiple levels of meaning at the same time. Symbols are multifaceted, meaning they have many sides or ways to be understood. Symbols don't just tell us to do something or to refrain from doing something. Symbols point to something beyond themselves. Symbols are able to communicate levels of meanings that lie far beyond the direct and immediate awareness of the people who interact with symbols.

"Symbol" is derived from the Greek word *symballein,* meaning "to throw together, to bring together, or to connect." The concrete meaning of this word goes back to the Greek custom of writing the name of friends on a shard or fragment of pottery. When the friends had to leave one another, the shard would be broken and each friend would take a piece. When they reunited, sometimes years later, their friendship was confirmed by the fact that the pieces that were brought together connected perfectly. A symbol works in a similar manner as it brings together different realities, visible ones and nonvisible ones, and connects them to form a meaning that is far beyond the visible reality.

A simple definition of a "symbol" is something that can be seen, heard, tasted, or felt by the human senses that calls forth another experience that is usually immaterial, not concrete, and cannot be sensed. In order for symbols to work, there needs to be a connection between the human experience of the symbol and the deeper reality they symbolize. We are, for instance, able to make connections between water and baptism because the cleansing power of water helps us understand baptism as a symbol for divine cleansing. Our human experience of the destructive power of water helps us to connect to water's ability to bring about death, which in turn connects to our participation

Baptism by immersion,
Cathedral of the Holy Angels, Los Angeles

in the death of Jesus. The fact that water sustains life and that life is born out of water also allows water to symbolize our new birth into the Church through the waters of baptism. Contrary to signs, symbols thus are not chosen arbitrarily.

Symbols also require a certain context in order to work. Water does not always function as a symbol. It only becomes a symbol in a liturgical context. When we use water for washing dishes, the water is nothing but dishwater. When we use it for bathing, it is nothing but bath water. But when we use water for baptism, it becomes a symbol that holds great meaning. During the celebration of the sacrament, water is no longer ordinary. It becomes baptismal water that cleanses us from sin and drowns us in the death of Jesus so we may rise with him again. Baptismal water is our entry into the Christian community. It births us into the Church. Contrary to signs, symbols only work within a specific context.

Although there is some learning involved when relating to symbols, there is also an immediacy that allows us to connect more quickly and directly. When we place our hand on a hot stove-top, we do not carefully process what is happening before removing our hand. Our reaction is direct and immediate. We quickly remove our hand! Symbols, especially primary symbols like water or fire, ought to inspire a similar reaction. Symbols communicate immediately and directly, but not everything is communicated at once. That is the beauty of symbols. Like all good relationships, there is a fullness to their meaning that continues to deepen over time. We discover more levels of meaning as we continue to encounter a symbol.

This complexity of meanings is the main difference between signs and symbols. Signs need to be extremely simple and clear, while symbols enjoy a level of ambiguity. Signs communicate one message, while symbols create a greater meaning that leads to a deeper understanding. Signs are used when there is not enough time to communicate a message in words, as with traffic signs. Symbols are often used when words cannot possibly suffice.

DAILY SYMBOLS AND SACRED SYMBOLS

One day, my fourteen-year-old niece proudly showed me her "promise" ring. She then told me about a boy in her class she liked very much. She understood that she was too young to date, but she was so pleased that he had given her this ring. When I asked her what the ring meant to her, she explained that it represented their promise to one another, and that one day they would get married.

I was moved by the innocence and even the naiveté of my niece, but I was also amazed at the layers of meaning that were heaped upon the simple string tied around her finger. It was a far cry from any engagement diamond that might signify a future marriage; however, as a symbol of a lofty promise it was very important to her.

We are all surrounded by symbols and use them on a daily basis as we struggle to express the inexpressible marvel at the birth of a baby, the depth of our love when celebrating a birthday or an anniversary, or the layers of deep emotions we experience when a loved one becomes ill or dies. In such situations, when we don't quite know what to say or when we fear our words will fall short, we reach for symbols. Even when we look for a card to accompany flowers, the card itself becomes a symbol of our feelings far beyond the printed words or any that we write by hand. The very act of giving the card becomes a symbol of care. Indeed, we are symbolic people, although we might not always be cognizant of this or aware of how we live out this reality in our daily lives.

When it comes to our faith, we use symbols even more readily to approach that which by definition cannot be explained or captured by words: the mysteries of creation and salvation. While science tries to explain certain aspects of these mysteries, symbols seek to reveal meaning as they invite us into an ever-deepening contemplation. The liturgy and the sacraments of the Catholic Church use symbols to share meaning and reveal deeper meaning. This is the language of symbols.

SACRED SYMBOLS AND SACRAMENTS

What Is a Sacrament?

The word "sacrament" comes from the Latin *sacramentum*. It was borrowed by early Christian writers from its pre-Christian use in the Roman army, where it referred to the binding relationship between a soldier and his commander. The unbreak-

The imposition of hands during an ordination to the priesthood

able relationship between the two was sealed by a *sacramentum* and consisted of an oath or pledge of fidelity sworn by the soldier to the commander. It also included a kind of branding by the commander on the soldier's body to indicate that he was bound to this particular commander until death. The Romans understood a *sacramentum* as both words and action that sealed a binding relationship.

Tertullian, one of the great early Christian writers, who died around the year 220 CE, borrowed this word when he described "initiation" as a *sacramentum* that consisted of an oath, which in this case was the profession of faith and baptismal formula, and a branding that occurred through water and oil.

Saint Augustine, who died in 430 CE, continued this practice when he described a *sacramentum* as a sacred sign or a visible word that included both a verbal and material element. This understanding eventually led to the distinction between matter, the material element present in a sacrament, such as bread and wine for the Eucharist, and the form, or verbal formula, such as the words, "receive the gifts of the Holy Spirit," as is used in the sacrament of confirmation. This pattern of matter and form characterizes each of our sacraments and continues to be present in the accompanying rituals until today, as we see in the current *Catechism of the Catholic Church*. The catechism defines a sacrament as an outward sign instituted by Christ to give grace.

The sacraments are efficacious signs of grace, instituted by Christ and entrusted to the Church, by which divine life is dispensed to us. The visible rites by which the sacraments are celebrated signify and make present the graces proper to each sacrament. They bear fruit in those who receive them with the required dispositions (Catechism of the Catholic Church, 1131).

There are seven sacraments, each with its own matter and form. The Church has also discovered a symbol that offers the matter or the material element connected with the sacrament.

They are as follows:

Baptism	water
Reconciliation	confession of sins and penance
Confirmation	oil of chrism
Eucharist	bread and wine
Anointing of the sick	oil of the sick and laying on of hands
Holy orders	the imposition of hands
Marriage	mutual consent of a couple to be married to one another

How Do Sacraments Make Use of Symbols?

Sacraments and symbols connect intimately with one another in the matter and form relationship. Symbols are the material aspect or the "form" of the sacrament. Each of the seven sacraments has its own matter and thus its own symbol. The matter and symbol for the sacraments of initiation, three sacraments by which we become full members of the Church, are water for baptism, oil of chrism for confirmation, and bread and wine for the Eucharist.

These sacramental symbols are meaningful because humans instinctively relate to symbols and because we relate to the symbols used in the sacraments on a presymbolic level in our daily life. Why is this so?

Humans have the capacity to be symbolic beings. Not only can we communicate with one another in a literal manner that already sets us apart from other life forms, we also communicate in a symbolic manner that sets us even more apart from other life forms, such as animals. We give flowers on Mother's Day and chocolate on Valentine's Day as a symbol of our love. We could more easily say, "I love you," and not buy presents, but somehow these gifts have become symbols that enhance and underline our vows of love in a way that make them more concrete. They are something we can touch and share to show our love more completely.

Sacramental symbols help us experience our faith more fully because we relate to them on a presymbolic or instinctive level that goes beyond our conscious thought. Oil is present everywhere in our lives. We use oil in our food, thus it has a nourishing aspect. We use oil to

*The elevation of
the Eucharist*

soothe and heal our skin when it is burnt, thus it has a healing aspect. Oil also harbors a destructive power with the ability to explode or spread fire. Thus oil has the ability to sustain life while it can also cause death. Our human experience of oil allows it to communicate the many forms of God's salvific work in the person and in the Church when it is used for two of the sacraments of initiation: baptism and confirmation, as well as for holy orders and the anointing of the sick.

FAITHFUL REFLECTIONS

Signs and symbols have been a part of our life since we were born. Although we might not notice it, we rely on many nonverbal elements of communication in our daily life. In our worship, our instinctive and presymbolic relationship with symbols allow us to connect with the sacramental symbols that have become part of the liturgical richness of Christian gatherings throughout history. The nonverbal elements that are a part of our Church symbols are important because they make up the matter for the celebration of the sacraments, beyond any words or form. I invite you to take some time to remember the relationships of faith and spirit and the nonverbal communication that have formed you as you consider these questions.

✦ *Think back to an important moment in your life, either of great joy or great sadness. What do you remember the most? Do you have mementos of those moments? How do you treat them?*

✦ *What are some symbols you have used to communicate with a loved one or shared with someone during times of sadness or joy or just because you wanted to do so?*

✦ *How have you experienced the power of symbols in the sacraments? What has been your favorite encounter? Why?*

CHAPTER TWO

FUNDAMENTAL SYMBOLS

One of my favorite vacations was spent in Montana. We stayed in a rustic cabin far away from any town and were surrounded by nature. We went to bed when it turned dark and got up as soon as the sun rose. We built fires to warm ourselves on chilly evenings and to cook meals. We dug vegetables in the dirt until our nails were black and our hands ached. We drew water from the creek and swam in the lake. The wind blew in our faces as we walked through the fields. There were no buttons to push for ice, faucets for hot water, or switches for light or music. Nothing was easy, but it was good to reconnect with the basic elements of earth: water, fire, air. These are the foundational building blocks of who we are and the earth on which we live.

One afternoon I was floating on my back in the lake and looking at the sky. Suddenly the beautiful blue turned black and torrential rains began to pour. I struggled mightily to get back to shore, but the power of water was real in all its magnificence and terror. At that moment I understood, more than ever before, why we use water for baptism. I had no problem imagining what it might be like to die and be buried in these churning waters.

Water, like fire and food, is one of the primary symbols in our liturgy. We connect to these symbols in a liturgical context because we have a presymbolic relationship with them outside the liturgy. We have been surrounded by these elements in the world and understand some of how they function. This enables us to connect to them on a basic and instinctive level in the liturgy. Often we have also been taught what these elements mean in the Bible and why particular symbols, such as bread and wine, are used in the sacraments. All of this information forms our understanding and helps us to connect more deeply with the primary symbols in the liturgy.

WATER

OUR PRESYMBOLIC HUMAN EXPERIENCE WITH WATER

As a child, I was terrified of water. I blame it on my swimming instructor, who grabbed me and threw me into the deep end of the pool when I appeared to hesitate taking the plunge. I thrashed and spluttered, and in the end made it out of the water upset but alive—and still afraid of water.

Although it might make sense to attribute my fear to this one traumatic experience, I suspect the root of my fear goes much deeper and connects to our shared human experience of water. All of us relate to water in one way or another. Whether we live in the swamps of Louisiana or the deserts of Nevada, we need water to survive. Water can kill us, either by its presence or absence. This is the power of water.

On the one hand, water is essential to all human life. Ninety percent of our bodies are made of water. We are conceived in water, and we are born out of water. We drink water. We use water to clean our homes and to cleanse ourselves. We relax while listening to water softly lapping on the river shore, and we get exhilarated when surfing a towering wave in the ocean.

Water is also a powerful agent of destruction. Low-lying areas near the ocean are at risk of tsunamis, while rivers often flood the plains. Both experiences leave paths of massive destruction and great human loss. However, the absence water is also destructive. A persistent drought parches crops and leads to cracked soil, a loss of food, and possible loss of life.

In sum, we need water to survive while that same water possesses the ability to kill us. It is precisely these diverse and contradictory human experiences with water that become presymbolic stepping-stones for us to encounter water as a liturgical and sacramental symbol.

BIBLICAL REFERENCES TO WATER

The Bible tells us of the power of water as a giver of life and agent of destruction in many different ways. Divine wrath is realized with water either against the chosen race or against an enemy. At the time of the great Flood, God allowed water to cover the whole earth: "The waters swelled so mightily on the earth that all the high mountains under the whole heaven were covered....And all flesh died that moved on the earth" (Genesis 7:19, 21). In order to save the Israelites, God let an entire army be swallowed up by water: "Then Moses stretched out his hand over the sea. The LORD drove the sea back by a strong east wind all night, and turned the sea into dry land; and the waters were divided...and at dawn the sea returned to its normal depth...and covered...the entire army" (Exodus 14:21, 27–28).

God gave water to the Israelites to quench their thirst. When they were on their long journey through the desert on the way to the Promised Land, God provided them with manna to eat and water to drink, "Then Moses lifted his hand and struck the rock twice with his staff; water came out abundantly, and the congregation and their livestock drank" (Numbers 20:11). The quenching of a more profound thirst is described by the prophet Isaiah when he writes how God invites all people to satisfy their thirst: "Everyone who thirsts, come to the waters" (Isaiah 55:1).

In the Bible, water is also used on many occasions for cleaning and especially for ritual cleansing: "When they go into the tent of meeting, or when they come near the altar to minister...they shall wash with water, so that they may not die" (Exodus 30:20).

Water, most importantly is shown to be a place of revelation and a source of salvation: "I baptize you with water for repentance, but one who is more powerful than I is coming after me....He will baptize you with the Holy Spirit and fire" (Matthew 3:11). Or, "and the eunuch said, 'Look, here is water! What is to prevent me from being baptized'" (Acts 8:36)?

WATER IN THE LITURGY

Water is used in the sacramental, liturgical, and devotional life of the Church in a variety of ways. The most profound and life-altering use of the symbol of water is in the sacrament of baptism. Our presymbolic experience with water prepares us well for the celebration of the sacramental experience of baptism as bath, burial, and birth.

In the same way that water is used to cleanse our bodies, the baptismal waters are used to cleanse our soul. Through their baptismal bath, the newly baptized, who are called neophytes or "new shoots," are washed from everything that stands between them and a perfect union with God. The baptismal waters cleanse the neophytes from all personal sins, as well as original sin.

We touch the water of the font to remind us of our baptism, St. Clare Church, O'Fallon, Illinois

Due to the potential of drowning in water, Saint Paul's account of dying with Christ in baptism in order to rise with him to new life is profoundly experienced through immersion in the baptismal waters. "Do you not know that all of us who have been baptized into Christ Jesus were baptized into his death" (Romans 6:3)? Water then becomes the place of the neophyte's symbolic death with Christ.

Because water is absolutely necessary to sustain life and because all life is conceived and born out of water, the baptismal font and in turn the baptismal waters become the place where the neophytes are born into the Church through the sacrament of baptism.

In addition to baptism, water is also used in blessings. Upon entering a church, people often dip their hands into the baptismal font or into a small holy water dish or container posted on a wall and bless themselves. This custom has a double purpose. It allows for the renewing of baptismal vows through the symbolic act of touching the water in the baptismal font and signing themselves with the sign of the cross. It is also a custom that was intended to ward off evil. All other blessings with holy water are intended to call down God's blessing on the people, animals, objects and places, and ward off evil.

FIRE

OUR PRESYMBOLIC HUMAN EXPERIENCE WITH FIRE

Since the beginning of human history, we have had a complex relationship with fire. At first, fire was treated with great deference and respect because it was not able to be created or controlled. Once humans discovered ways to make fire and control it, our relationship with fire changed to one of utilization for production, cooking, protection, warmth, and any number of uses. Nevertheless, even today fire remains one of our best friends and is at the same time one of our fiercest adversaries.

Who does not love the crackling and dancing of fire in an outdoor fire pit? Throughout history, generations have been raised sitting around campfires all over the world, telling stories, and singing songs. Fire provides us with heat and light, a cozy fireplace by which to read during the dark of winter, and comfort against cold and dampness. We use fire to boil water and cook our meals, clear fields, and fertilize the soil. Fire possesses many life-giving qualities.

On the other hand, fire has the power to destroy and kill. Forest fires devastate thousands of acres of trees and plants each year, killing animals, and sometimes people. The horror of a rushing brushfire or of being trapped in a burning house is unimaginable. While fire helps us thrive and survive, it can threaten our very existence. This paradox of fire and light parallels the life-and-death mystery present in its symbolic and sacramental use.

BIBLICAL REFERENCES TO FIRE

The Bible is filled with descriptions of how fire destroys, inspires, guides, and enlightens. Among the many stories of fire, some stand out. God uses the destructive power of fire to show anger and cause ruin: "The LORD rained on Sodom and Gomorrah sulphur and fire from the LORD out of heaven" (Genesis 19:24). God used fire for a divine epiphany: "There the angel of the LORD appeared to him in a flame of fire out of a bush; he looked, and the bush was blazing, yet it was not consumed" (Exodus 3:2). God also used fire by night to guide the people: "The LORD went in front of them in a pillar of cloud by day, to lead them along the way, and in a pillar of fire by night, to give them light, so that they might travel by day and by night" (Exodus 13:21). Finally, God's spirit is manifested in fire that comes down on the apostles, "Divided tongues, as of fire, appeared among them, and a tongue rested on each of them" (Acts 2:3).

FIRE IN THE LITURGY

Without question, the blessing of the Easter fire and the lighting of the paschal candle from the Easter fire are some of most powerful symbols of the whole liturgical year. However, they are also the least experienced, since not everyone is able to attend the vigil each year or even knows that it is being celebrated. Imagine being in front of a church where those who will be initiated into the faith and their sponsors are gathered around the fire as it is being prepared.

They watch as wood is placed in a twelve-foot-wide fire pit and begins to burn in the cool darkness. As the fire burns and grows, so does the gathering of people surrounding it, then at the height of its flame, the priest blesses this fire from which the new Easter candle will be lit.

The origin of the Easter fire predates Christianity to when people lit fires to mark the cycle of the sun and moon for the winter and summer solstice, as well as the spring and fall equinox. The same instinctive, presymbolic experience of fire that led people to use it to mark these moments also inspired Christians to use fire and light as a symbol of Christ, the true light amid darkness.

While a large fire is only present once a year in the liturgy, candles are lit at all liturgical services. The primary candle is the Easter or paschal candle that is lit from the Easter fire and symbolizes the light of Christ that destroys all darkness. The lighting of the paschal candle sparks the acclaim that Christ is our light. The assembly in turn lights smaller candles from the Christ light as they share in his gift and mission to bring light to the world.

Whether small or large, the flame of faith is remembered whenever candles or fire are present in worship. People light candles in religious shrines to symbolize their continued prayers to God. Sometimes candles are lit at home as symbols of our ongoing prayer and devotion to God, Mary, and the saints. In all of these settings, our presymbolic instincts are at work drawing us to fire in order for our faith to be enkindled as we become enwrapped in the power of symbol.

OIL

OUR PRESYMBOLIC HUMAN EXPERIENCE WITH OIL

Olive trees are one of my favorite trees. They are extremely resilient, beautiful with their gnarled trunks and olive-green leaves, and have a long lifespan. Although they do not bear cold, they can withstand long droughts to live hundreds and even thousands of years. It is mind-boggling to think that some of the olive trees in the Garden of Olives where Jesus prayed the night before he died might still be standing as silent witnesses to the events of that night.

Not only do I love olive trees, but like millions of people, I delight in its fruit. The smell of fresh virgin olive oil—cold or simmering in a pan waiting for garlic to be added—is a delight for the senses. And who can resist the taste of good olive oil drizzled over beautiful tomato slices and basil leaves?

Of course, many kinds of vegetables provide oil. There are also animal oils and fossil fuels, such as petroleum. Some oils are prized for their culinary qualities, others are used to soothe our skin when it cracks in the winter or burns in summer. Scented oils provide shine to our hair, perfume our bodies, and arouse our senses. Oil is also used to light lamps, fuel cars, and heat our homes. For better or worse, oil has become an essential component of our daily lives.

Oil can also be damaging. Some oils found in our food can be detrimental to our physical health and should only be eaten in moderation. Frying with oil can produce burn injuries. Oil slicks in our oceans and rivers have created disasters. And oil from our cars can poison our atmosphere.

Our presymbolic relationship with oil today is complex and far removed from the simplicity that inspired early Christians to use it as a liturgical symbol. Nevertheless, when liberated from today's complexities, we still deeply connect to the experiences of the people of God in biblical times, when most of the oil came from the olive trees that still dot the Mediterranean and Middle Eastern landscapes.

The anointing of an altar

BIBLICAL REFERENCES TO OIL

Like other fundamental symbols, oil is used in multiple ways in the Bible. It was first used to symbolize God's presence with people in their time of need. Oil thus became a symbol of God's soothing and healing presence: "Therefore God, your God, has anointed you with the oil of gladness beyond your companions; your robes are all fragrant with myrrh and aloes and cassia. From ivory palaces stringed instruments make you glad" (Psalm 45:7–8). Or, "Then I bathed you [Jerusalem] with water and washed off the blood from you, and anointed you with oil" (Ezekiel 16:9).

Oil was also used to affirm God's presence with those who were appointed priest, prophet, and king. Aaron, for example, was anointed priest: "You shall take the anointing-oil, and pour it on his head and anoint him [Aaron]" (Exodus 29:7). David was anointed as king: "Then Samuel took the horn of oil, and anointed him in the presence of his brothers; and the spirit of the LORD came mightily upon David from that day forward" (1 Samuel 16:13). Elisha was anointed as prophet: "You shall anoint Jehu son of Nimshi as king over Israel; and you shall anoint Elisha son of Shaphat of Abel-meholah as prophet in your place" (I Kings 19:16).

Humans also used oil in sacrifices during biblical times, similar to their use of animal offerings: "Jacob rose early in the morning, and he took the stone that he had put under his head and set it up for a pillar and poured oil on the top of it" (Genesis 28:18). They also use oil to heal and sooth: "They cast out many demons, and anointed with oil many who were sick and cured them" (Mark 6:13). Or, "He went to him and bandaged his wounds, having poured oil and wine on them" (Luke 10:34). Finally, humans used oil to honor the body after death: "The women who had come with him from Galilee followed, and they saw the tomb and how his body was laid. Then they returned, and prepared spices and ointments" (Luke 23:55–56).

OIL IN THE LITURGY

Oil is used as the matter or material aspect for four of our seven sacraments: baptism, confirmation, holy orders (the ordination of priests and bishops), and in the anointing of the sick. Oil is also used for the dedication of altars and churches. These uses are patterned on both our presymbolic experience of oil, as well as biblical rituals.

The anointing of the sick

The permeating quality of oil symbolizes how the Spirit permeates those who are being anointed and strengthens them for the task at hand, such as living the Christian life in the case of confirmation, or serving as a priest or bishop. The healing quality of oil provides an additional reason for its use in the anointing of the sick. The biblical use of oil in the anointing of priests, prophets, and kings also offers a theological foundation for its use in our sacraments.

There are three different oils that are used in the sacramental life of the Church: 1) the oil of the catechumens for the baptism of infants and for adults preparing for initiation; 2) the oil of the sick for the anointing of the sick; and 3) sacred chrism for the baptism of infants, confirmation, holy orders, and during the consecration of churches and altars.

BREAD AND WINE

OUR PRESYMBOLIC HUMAN EXPERIENCE WITH BREAD AND WINE

It has been many years since my grandmother hosted her weekly Sunday dinners. They were great occasions for our extended family to get together and share our lives with one another while enjoying a lovely meal. In addition to the Sunday dinners, my immediate family customarily shared two daily meals as we were growing up. Breakfast was somewhat on the run, but lunch and dinner were organized affairs where every member of our family sat together around the dining room table.

Our family dinners were always memorable, not only because of the food we shared but also because of our conversations and the time we spent together. Looking back, I realize what a luxury it was to have that time together in the same place and the resources to buy the food we were blessed to enjoy with one another. While our eating rituals were important to me and a building block of our close-knit family, food and drink are also some of the most basic needs we share as human beings. Without them, we simply cannot survive. Today a trip to a farmer's market or a stop at the bakery or butcher shop is a way to stay in touch with local sources. It was not all that long ago that much of humanity's time was focused on actual farming, gathering, and hunting. In fact, millions of people throughout the world are still dependent on these tasks today.

Because we have a deep presymbolic connection with breaking bread and drinking wine, the link to the sacramental and symbolic use of bread and wine can be made easily. Bread is still a staple of most daily meals in many cultures. It can take the form of basic bread as well as luxurious baked goods for festive occasions. Though the act of breaking bread is often abandoned in favor of buying sliced bread, breaking bread still lingers in our common experience. Whole loaves can easily be found in bakeries, and the temptation to break off a piece of a freshly baked baguette is very real.

The drinking of wine has also been a centuries-long part of many cultures. Wine has been ascribed medicinal qualities: It was used to settle an upset stomach and to clean out wounds. Still, the principal quality of wine is to add festivity to a gathering and emphasize unity among those who share the cup. Although current practices dictate that each guest has his own glass at dinner parties, this was not always the case. The custom of sharing a common cup among table guests has a long history both as part of sharing meals together and at other gatherings.

BIBLICAL REFERENCES TO FOOD

The Bible uses bread in many contexts, ranging from basic food, to ritual food, to spiritual nourishment. In the Old Testament, bread was offered to guests as a sign of hospitality: "He urged them strongly, so they turned aside to him and entered his house; and he made them a feast, and baked unleavened bread, and they ate" (Genesis 19:3). Unleavened bread was used in rituals and became a sign of the covenant between God and the people of Israel: "Seven days you shall eat unleavened bread; on the first day you shall remove leaven from your houses, for whoever eats leavened bread from the first day until the seventh day shall be cut off from Israel" (Exodus 12:15).

In the New Testament, Jesus used bread to refer to all earthly food. He also used bread to reveal his divinity. Finally, he used bread as a symbol of divine nourishment and as a symbol of his own body broken for our salvation. Saint Paul used bread as a symbol of the entire body of Christ, the Church. When Jesus taught his disciples to pray the one perfect prayer, he included the following petition: "Give us this day our daily bread" (Matthew 6:11). In this instance, bread symbolizes earthly food. In the miracle of the multiplication of the bread, Jesus revealed himself as the Son of God: "Then Jesus took the loaves, and when he had given thanks, he distributed them to those who were seated; so also the fish, as much as they wanted. When they were satisfied, he told his disciples, 'Gather up the fragments left over, so that nothing may be lost.' So they gathered them up, and from the fragments of the five barley loaves, left by those who had eaten, they filled twelve baskets" (John 6:11–13). Jesus also used bread when he explained to his disciples that he is spiritual food that will leave us satisfied forever: "I am the living bread that came down from heaven. Whoever eats of this bread will live for ever" (John 6:51). Jesus also talked about bread when referring to his sacrifice the night before he died: "While they were eating, Jesus took a loaf of bread, and after blessing it he broke it, gave it to the disciples, and said, 'Take, eat; this is my body'" (Matthew 26:26). Finally, Saint Paul used bread to speak about the unity of the Church, the body of Christ: "Because there is one bread, we who are many are one body, for we all partake of the one bread" (1 Corinthians 10:17).

Though there are many reprimands against drinking too much wine in the Old Testament, there are also many references to wine as a sign of celebration and a source of joy: "You cause the grass to grow for the cattle, and plants for people to use to bring forth food from the earth, and wine to gladden the human heart, oil to make the face shine, and bread to strengthen the human heart" (Psalm 104:14–15). And, "Go, eat your bread with enjoyment, and drink your wine with a merry heart; for God has long ago approved what you do" (Ecclesiastes 9:7). Sometimes wine was used in reference to the heavenly banquet: "On this mountain the LORD of hosts will make for all peoples a feast of rich food, a feast of well-matured wines, of rich food filled with marrow, of well-matured wines strained clear" (Isaiah 25:6).

In the New Testament, wine was also used in the context of celebration, as at the wedding of Cana. Through this miracle of changing water into wine at Cana, Jesus used this first miracle to reveal himself as the Son of God: "Jesus did this, the first of his signs, in Cana of Galilee and revealed his glory; and his disciples believed in him" (John 2:11). Most importantly, Jesus used wine at the Last Supper as the symbol of his own blood that he would shed for our salvation. "Then he took a cup, and after giving thanks he gave it to them, saying, 'Drink from it, all of you; for this is my blood of the covenant, which is poured out for many for the forgiveness of sins" (Matthew 26:27). In his writings, Saint Paul used many occasions to affirm the truth that when we drink from the eucharistic cup we

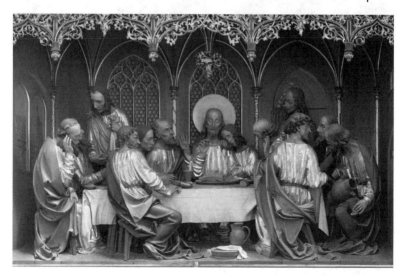

share in the Blood of Christ: "The cup of blessing that we bless, is it not a sharing in the blood of Christ? The bread that we break, is it not a sharing in the body of Christ" (1 Corinthians 10:16)? Or in the extended narration of the Last Supper: "For I received from the Lord what I also handed on to you, that the Lord Jesus on the night when he was betrayed took a loaf of bread, and when he had given thanks, he broke it and said, 'This is my body that is for you. Do this in remembrance of me.' In the same way he took the cup also, after supper, saying, 'This cup is the new covenant in my blood. Do this, as often as you drink it, in remembrance of me.' For as often as you eat this bread and drink the cup, you proclaim the Lord's death until he comes. Whoever, therefore, eats the bread or drinks the cup of the Lord in an unworthy manner will be answerable for the body and blood of the Lord" (1 Corinthians 11:23–27).

BREAD AND WINE IN THE LITURGY

Bread and wine are used for the celebration of the sacrament of the Eucharist, which is both the culmination of the sacraments of initiation and a sacrament we celebrate as weekly nourishment on our journey of faith.

After discerning and preparing to become a full member in the Church, those who have celebrated the sacraments of baptism and confirmation are welcomed to the table of the Lord. In the same way that a family table symbolizes unity among all those seated around it, the altar table in the church is reserved for those who are members of the community. However, the altar table symbolizes not only unity among those gathered around it but also the sacrifice Jesus made for us, as well as our willingness to face the same sacrifice if we are asked to do so.

FAITHFUL REFLECTIONS

God's presence is so extravagant that it flows through nature, our daily lives, and into the faith and rituals that we share together. We are able to connect with the fundamental liturgical symbols of water, fire, light, oil, bread, and wine because we encounter and use them in our daily lives. These presymbolic experiences stay with us as we read about these symbols in Scripture and experience them in our worship. While we can seem to learn more about the meaning of symbols by reading about them, we might do well to immerse ourselves in the elements at hand. What would it be like to set aside some time each week to experience water in a new way, light a candle during our prayer at home, rub oil on our skin, break bread rather than slice it, and toast God's presence with good wine? This is the surface of the celebration of symbols that awaits your experience.

✦ *How do you relate to water? What do you think about when you bless yourself upon entering the church?*

✦ *What is your strongest memory of fire or light? How does that impact your experience of fire and light in the liturgy?*

✦ *What liturgical symbol is most meaningful to you? What made it meaningful? What symbol would you like to have more meaning?*

CHAPTER THREE

SACRED ARCHITECTURE
AS SYMBOL

On October 28, 1944, Winston Churchill gave a now-famous speech during the rebuilding of the war-ravaged House of Commons. In it, he solemnly stated that, "We shape our dwellings, and afterwards our dwellings shape us." In 1960, *Time* magazine translated this phrase as, "We shape our buildings; thereafter they shape us." This idea has remained present in modern-day thought in a profound way that continues to point to this architectural truth. Although we design and build all our buildings, be they public or private, sacred or secular, they, in turn, shape us once they are built. Not only that, but they continue to impact successive generations.

Cathedral of St. Michael and St. Gudule, Brussels

Saint Peter's Basilica, Rome

Although we might think that church buildings express only the theology of a certain age and enable the liturgy of a certain time, we underestimate their formidable ability. Styles of architecture continue to impress their meaning and convey the liturgical theology for which they were built long after that age and time have passed. We can see this dynamic present in the architecture of Saint Peter's Basilica in Rome. Saint Peter's Basilica was built to honor Saint Peter, first among the apostles and martyr for the faith. Emperor Constantine erected the first basilica above what was believed to be Peter's tomb in the fourth century. By the end of the fifteenth century, however, the first basilica had fallen into such disrepair that a new basilica was built. Planning began in 1505, and the basilica was built by 1625. We encounter this basilica today.

Though a visitor might not realize it, the architecture of Saint Peter's directs them to the main altar erected above Saint Peter's tomb. This guidance begins at the plaza in front of Saint Peter's Basilica, where the arms of sculpture, Gian Lorenzo Bernini's colonnade, draws all who enter into a mystical journey toward the tomb of Saint Peter. Majestic stairs lead from the piazza outside to the grand portico of the basilica, where stately doors lead into the nave. Once inside, our eyes are drawn to the baldachin or canopy built over the high altar right above the Saint Peter's tomb. Even visitors who do not realize that Saint Peter is buried there are still guided to that very place. Indeed, we shape our architecture, and in turn it shapes and guides us.

A BRIEF HISTORY OF CHURCH ARCHITECTURE

Entrance portal at The Cathedral Basilica of Saint Denis, Paris

For some 2,000 years, we have built churches that express our faith, serve our liturgy, and inspire devotion. The result is a collection of buildings and art of unparalleled beauty and a history of church architecture that is both impressive and complex. It is impressive because it gives us a collection of buildings and art of unparalleled beauty. It is complex because it is the result of an ongoing search for the best possible way to house the faithful as they pray, grow in their faith, and live as the body of Christ in the world.

In a way, church architecture could be called a work in progress. It loves its rich past and learns from it. It seeks to be informed by the present. And it looks toward the future with great hope for better things to come. Church architecture reveals an ongoing dialogue among architecture and art, liturgy, and faith. This relationship is at times freeing because of the support and wider expression of faith that is welcomed by the Church, and at times confining as the Church shifts from fostering new expressions of church art and architecture to prescribing strict directives for the construction and decoration of churches.

Christian architecture began modestly. Early Christians prayed in

Basilica of St. Francis Xavier, Dryersville, Iowa

Jewish synagogues and gathered in private homes. They baptized where there was water, be that outside in a stream or in Roman baths. Existing architecture provided, at the most, a shelter for Christians at worship, rather than a place of prayer to call their own. As the Christian communities grew, particular houses were designated as house churches and were adapted to accommodate worship and other church needs. Some good examples of how the liturgical needs of the early third century dictated the refurbishing of houses are found in the house church at Dura-Europos, (235 CE) and at an early third-century house church in Rome known as the *titulus Equitii*.

With the conversion of the Roman Empire to Christianity through the Peace of Constantine (313 CE), Christians were allowed to worship publicly. This change drastically impacted Christian theology, its liturgy, and architecture. It was no longer sufficient for architecture to simply shelter and accommodate the liturgy. Buildings needed to make a theological and even a political statement. From that moment on, Christians discovered how to effectively use the formative power of architecture to express their faith. The Constantinian basilicas, such as the first Saint Peter's, the Carolinian and Romanesque churches, the great Gothic cathedrals, the magnificent Renaissance, Baroque and Rococo churches all have their own history and specific liturgical, theological—and sometimes political—messages that they have conveyed for centuries and still impress upon those who enter them today, despite vast changes in theology and liturgical styles.

Nineteenth- and early-twentieth-century church architects were at a loss for their own meaning system, so they borrowed from the glorious Christian past and adopted architectural expressions that held enough theological meaning to carry past forms into the next century. Byzantine, Romanesque, and Gothic revivals all illustrate a yearning for a church, a theology, and a liturgy of the past. The mere imitation of architectural style was presumed to restore that which was thought to be lost.

Since the beginning of the twentieth century, liturgists and architects alike have engaged in a search for a true revival. This revival was not merely one of style but of essential Christian truths that were translated into common languages, expressed in authentic liturgy, and celebrated in meaningful buildings. This fascinating journey has produced churches that may be different in material, style, and scope, but they share similar areas, such as the gathering place, the place for baptism, the place for the celebration of the Eucharist, the place for the reservation of the Eucharist, the place for reconciliation, and the sacristy.

Indoor gathering space at St. Clare Church, O'Fallon, Illinois

THE GATHERING PLACE

The gathering space is a place of transition from the secular world and the parking lot into God's world. Worshipers enter the gathering place having come from their homes, their workplace, or their vacation cabins. They have not seen one another in about a week. They are excited to share stories about their lives and are not quite ready for the liturgy. The gathering area helps people to transition from home to church, from daily business to the liturgy, from all that is profane to all that is sacred. This transition is not always easy. The process really begins as we ready ourselves for church and make our way there. Historically, church buildings have always had these sorts of transitional spaces because builders knew that it takes time for us to wind down and become accustomed to the sacred. Gathering spaces have taken different shapes and forms over the centuries. The great Mediterranean basilicas of the fourth century have courtyards and porticos that ease the transition. The celebrated medieval cathedrals have plazas and narthexes that allow for transitional encounters and conversations. Many of today's churches are incorporating dedicated space for gathering and transition into their building plans. In some of these churches, the baptismal font is located in the gathering place, symbolizing that in the sacrament of baptism we transition from our pre-Christian life to membership in the Church.

Outdoor gathering space, Cathedral of St. John the Evangelist, Milwaukee

Baptismal font, Our Lady of Lourdes, Houston

THE PLACE FOR BAPTISM

Baptism is the first of the seven sacraments of the Catholic Church. It is the sacrament that incorporates us into the body of Christ, the Church, and is the entryway to the other sacraments. The main characteristics of baptism can be understood through these three images: baptismal bath, baptismal burial, and baptismal birth. In baptism, we are washed clean from everything that prevents perfect union with God, who claims us as an adopted child. In baptism we are buried with Christ so we may rise with him on the last day. Through the waters of baptism, we are born into the Church, the body of Christ.

At first, Christians baptized wherever there was water, which was mostly in rivers. However, by the beginning of the third century, small baptismal tubs were used in house churches that served the small Christian communities. After Christianity became the religion of the Roman Empire in the fourth century, bigger places for baptism were required, so public baths were used. These public baths inspired the construction of baptisteries, the first buildings built exclusively to house the sacrament of baptism. These first baptisteries were large buildings with elaborate decorations emphasizing the importance of baptism. The baptismal fonts that occupied the better part of the main section of these buildings were large and filled with water to allow for the full immersion of adults.

By the seventh century, however, several important shifts took place. The doctrine of original sin resulted in a desire for parents to have their children baptized as soon as possible after birth. In addition, more of an emphasis was placed on the effect of the sacrament rather

Font in the San Fernando Cathedral, San Antonio

than on how the child was baptized, so a minimal experience of the symbol, such as using only a little water, came to be common and eroded the full experience of water, so much so that the custom of immersion was eventually replaced with the pouring of a little bit of water on the child's head. The final shift sought to cover and lock fonts because holy water was used for witchcraft, and fear abounded around the threat of it being stolen. As a result of these changes, baptismal fonts became smaller and smaller and were locked up in a side chapel near the entrance of the church. Elaborate covers protected the water from being seen and touched outside of the celebration of the sacrament. The place for baptism was thus moved from its own building into the church proper, and the font structure changed from a large in-ground immersion vessel to one that could be held on a pedestal.

In light of the Second Vatican Council, the Church rediscovered the way baptism was celebrated in the early Church, and a number of its aspects were brought back into practice. The Rite of Christian Initiation of Adults was reintroduced and became specifically designed for the preparation and initiation of adults. Baptism by immersion again became the norm and was to be done in the presence of the community, since baptism is the sacrament where the baptized join the Church. As a result, the place for baptism is located so that it is visible to the entire assembly in many contemporary or renovated churches. The fonts are also bigger in order to contain more water and allow for adult immersion.

Baptismal font, Chapel of Christ the Teacher, Portland University, Portland, Oregon

THE PLACE FOR RECONCILIATION

Before the Second Vatican Council, the sacrament of reconciliation was known as the sacrament of confession. The difference between the two is that the former emphasizes the act of confessing sins, while the latter emphasizes the experience of healing and reconciliation with God and with the Church.

Before the revision of the sacrament, the confessional was the place where we went to confess our sins for confession. The confessional was set up in such a way that it protected the identity of the confessor and quickly moved the sacrament along. In many churches, the confessional accommodated one person kneeling on either side of the priest so that when he finished praying with one person, the next

in line could confess as another got ready on the other side to do the same. Many churches still have their confessionals constructed in just this way, often because the architectural form has historical or artistic value; however, most of them are no longer used.

Today the place for reconciliation is known as the reconciliation chapel rather than a confessional. These chapels are less intimidating than confessionals and emphasize that the sacrament is to be a positive experience, highlighting healing rather than a punitive experience dwelling on our sinfulness. Reconciliation rooms are to be set up so the sacrament can be celebrated in direct conversation with the priest or anonymously behind a screen. A Bible is often present in the reconciliation chapel so that reading from

Top: Confessional, The Basilica of Saint Mary, Minneapolis
Bottom: Reconciliation chapel, The Basilica of Saint Mary, Minneapolis

Scripture can be part of the celebration, as is suggested in the rite. A crucifix and candles may also be present to enhance the celebration and experience of prayer. As a whole, the chapels are to be a place of renewal that will offer refreshment for the penitent and revive them on their journey of faith so they may live the life that God offers them more fully. The architecture of the reconciliation space and all that is contained in the chapel should support this experience of freedom from sin and reclaimed oneness with God.

Church of Saint Peter, Mendota, Minnesota

THE PLACE FOR THE CELEBRATION OF THE EUCHARIST

The Eucharist is the third of the three sacraments of initiation. It is also the only sacrament of initiation that can and should be repeated. This is why the entire body of Christ, the Church, gathers each Sunday to celebrate Eucharist. The Eucharist comprises two main sections: the Liturgy of the Word and the Liturgy of the Eucharist. In the Liturgy of the Word, we are nourished by the word that is proclaimed and expanded upon in the homily. In the Liturgy of the Eucharist, we are nourished by the Body and Blood of Christ.

The congregation, the ministers, and the two essential parts of the Eucharist inform how the building that accommodates this celebration should be designed. First and foremost, the building needs to accommodate the full, active, and conscious participation in the celebration of the Eucharist by all who are present. This means the space needs to allow for the entire assembly to see and hear the parts of the eucharistic celebration and participate in such ritual postures as kneeling, standing, sitting, and processing. Provisions should also be made for people who use walkers and wheelchairs to be part of the fullness of the celebration.

Some members of the community have specific liturgical roles, such as the priest celebrant, the deacons, the lectors, the psalmist, and the servers. A special place is reserved for them in our churches so they may exercise their ministry as well as possible. This dedicated area is referred to as the sanctuary and comes from the Latin word *sanctus,* meaning "holy." In most cases, the sanctuary is raised and houses the ambo (sometimes referred to as a lectern), the altar, and the celebrant's chair. The two major parts of the Eucharist, the Liturgy of the Word and the Liturgy of the Eucharist, take place respectively around the ambo and the altar in the sanctuary area. As a result, they are often located in close proximity to one another, although newer churches may locate them to be more removed from one another, to reinforce that each area is for a separate part of the liturgy. However, they should still be visually connected, built of similar materials, and complement one another in style.

Although it is not part of the celebration of the Eucharist, the tabernacle that houses the Blessed Sacrament is sometimes located in the sanctuary. This is especially the case in older churches, where the tabernacle is part of a former high altar. Other churches may have a special chapel that is dedicated to reserve the Blessed Sacrament, so the tabernacle will be located there.

Blessed Sacrament chapel, St. Mary's Cathedral of the Immaculate Conception, Portland, Oregon

THE PLACE FOR THE RESERVATION OF THE EUCHARIST

Dove container for the Eucharist, Bethany Chapel of the Archdiocese of Boston Pastoral Center

During the first ten centuries of the Church, the Blessed Sacrament was primarily reserved for communion of the sick and especially of those who were dying. It was believed that no one should make the great journey of faith to the next life without having been nourished by the Body of Christ, the food for the journey, viaticum. There was no common or prescribed place for reservation during these first thousand years, so it may have been reserved in the home where the priest lived or in one of the rooms adjacent to the church. It is certain, however, that the Blessed Sacrament was not reserved in the main part of the church.

The manner of reservation was also quite diverse. The earliest containers for reservation may have been simple wooden boxes. These became more complex as time went on, and by the tenth century the most popular container was in the shape of a dove that hung in the sanctuary. Another common shape was that of a tower, known as the sacraments tower, also located in the sanctuary.

It was not until after the Council of Trent, in the mid-sixteenth century, that more churches began reserving the Blessed Sacrament in the middle of the altar. Although this practice was encouraged, many churches and cathedrals in Europe preserved the tradition of reserving the Eucharist in a special chapel far in back of the altar in the apse, or in a side chapel. This is still the practice in many cathedrals in Europe, including Saint Peter's Basilica in Rome.

In the United States, most churches built before Vatican II have a tabernacle on the main altar of the church. Churches built after the council or those that have been renovated since then often have a special chapel that has been designed for the reservation of the

Blessed Sacrament or one that accommodates prayer before the Blessed Sacrament, either reserved in the tabernacle or exposed in the monstrance.

The *GIRM* calls for the Eucharist to be reserved in accordance with the structure of each church and legitimate local custom in a "tabernacle in a part of the church that is truly noble, prominent, conspicuous, worthily decorated, and suitable for prayer." The Eucharist should not be reserved on the altar that is used for the celebration of the Eucharist, however, and only one tabernacle should be present in each church. The tabernacle may be placed either in the main sanctuary or in a chapel "suitable for the private adoration and prayer of the faithful [128] and organically connected to the church and readily noticeable by the Christian faithful" (*GIRM* 314, 315).

THE SACRISTY

Although given a somewhat lofty name, the sacristy is, in essence, a work area used to prepare to celebrate the liturgy. "Sacristy" comes from the Latin word *sacer,* which means "sacred." The sacristy is the place where sacred objects are stored, cleaned, and maintained. It is also the place where ministers get ready before the liturgy. In some churches, these two functions have resulted in two different sacristies:

a working sacristy and a vesting sacristy. However, in most churches, both functions are housed in the same area.

Many objects used in the liturgy are cared for in the sacristy. The vestments that priests and deacons wear are stored

Sacristy, The Basilica of Saint Mary, Minneapolis

there, as are the albs or cassock and surplices worn by the altar servers. The sacred vessels—such as the chalices and patens—are stored, cleaned, and polished in the sacristy. It is also the place where other liturgical objects, such as the aspergillum, or sprinkling branch, and the thurible are kept. This means that sacristies often include a safe to store such items as valuable gold vessels and a sink for general use. Sacristies must also include a sacrarium. Again, the Latin word *sacer* or "sacred" is the root for this word. The sacrarium is a special sink that drains directly into the ground, rather than draining into the sewer system. It is used for the washing of the sacred vessels after they have been purified. However, any precious blood that is left in the cups should be consumed. It is never to be poured into the sacrarium. The water used to purify the chalice and communion cups is also to be consumed. Only the water used for washing, after the purification, may be poured into the sacrarium.

As mentioned, the sacristy is also the place where ministers ready themselves for the liturgy. This can, on occasion, turn the sacristy into a noisy and somewhat busy place right before the liturgy. Eucharistic ministers are confirming they know where to stand. A lector is in a corner reviewing the reading. Servers are putting on albs and jostling one another. The sacristan is trying to make sure everything and everyone is in the right place for liturgy to begin. This is not an easy space in which to prepare mentally or spiritually for anything, thus it is sometimes helpful to have separate areas for these functions. This bustling activity was not always a standard part of the sacristy ambiance. Priests used to quietly recite prayers while putting on their vestments to help them prepare for the celebration. In some sacristies, cards with these prayers are still present, or you can see them in the window above the priest's vesting table.

Sacristy at St. Mary's Cathedral, Sydney

Although there are many details to attend to and many more people involved in preparing for Mass today, we might do well to reclaim the silence and prayerfulness of the sacristy from years past. A prayer by all ministers before Mass begins would help. It will not only quiet everyone down, it will also focus all the ministers on the sacred tasks they are about to begin.

FAITHFUL REFLECTIONS

Do you remember praying in the home where you grew up as a child? Did you have a favorite place to pray? Sometimes we long for our favorite prayer setting when we are attracted to a particular style of church architecture. Sometimes we seek just the opposite. Think back and imagine receiving the sacrament of reconciliation and the Eucharist for the first time. Think about what drew you to church and what compelled you to stay as you grew older. What images stand out that created a good experience for you? Was it the architecture? Was it the priest? The choir? The hospitality? What kind of church would you build if you had free rein and possibility? Draw or describe your ideal church or think about where you currently worship. What would you change?

✦ *Does your church have a place for gathering? What is your experience of gathering as you arrive for worship? What creates this experience?*

✦ *Where is your church's baptismal font located? What is its shape and size? Does it allow for a full experience of baptism? What does it express by its shape, size, and location?*

✦ *Is the place for reconciliation in your church inviting? How does the space affect your experience of the sacrament?*

CHAPTER FOUR

SACRED ART
AS SYMBOL

A local contemporary art museum once asked me to give a Catholic tour of an exhibit titled "Ultra-Baroque." I accepted the invitation because I recognized the word "Baroque" and thought it would be easy to do, since by background I am a Catholic art historian. When I received the catalog of the exhibit, however, I was surprised to find that the exhibit showed abstract art from South America, with only faint allusions to Baroque art as it was celebrated in South America three or more centuries earlier.

As I visited the exhibit to prepare for my tour, I found myself in front of a work titled *Milagros* ("miracles"). Though abstract, it was beautiful and compelling. It reminded me of

Cuadro of the Nativity, Pamplona Alta, Peru

Frederick Hart, Cross of the Millennium, (1/3 life-size),1992, clear acrylic resin © Chesley LLC

the Catholic custom to bring the image of a failing body part to a sacred place, such as a Marian shrine, and leave it there while praying for a miraculous cure. As I stood mesmerized by this work of art, my mobile phone rang. My sister told me that my dad was having emergency surgery. In an instant, this museum that was dedicated to modern art became a sacred place for me as I prayed for a miracle and continued to be inspired by *Milagros*.

This contemporary work of art, which was not intended to inspire prayer, all of a sudden did just that. To be sure, neither the setting nor the art was intended to be religious. However, the element of the sacred that is present in all good art and which connects us with the divine creative power came to the surface to inspire me with hope and courage. Even though *Milagros* was created to mean one thing, it evoked a new meaning in me far beyond the intentions of the artist.

Because good art is born out of the artist's connectedness with divine creative power, it can communicate in ways that are neither intended by the artist nor foreseen by the art critic. Good art can thus communicate in unexpected ways, beyond word or thought, revealing a deeper meaning. This kind of communication occurs when a true encounter occurs between the art and the beholder. This kind of experience is not often the result of a lengthy thought process or an exercise to dissect the meaning of the art. It is more like falling in love. We don't reason ourselves into falling in love. It just happens, and all of a sudden, we know. Art can work in a similar way. It does not explain, rather it reveals and can do so in unexpected ways and in unexpected places, such as in an art museum. The art, the location, and the circumstances often come together, unplanned, when encounters of this kind take place.

For several months I had been walking by a crucifix created by Frederick Hart. It was displayed in the window of a local art gallery, and I noticed it each time I walked by the gallery. I did not think I liked it because it was made of acrylic, and normally I do not like acrylic sculptures. Despite that, I kept returning to the gallery to see it. It was as if the cross drew me back to itself quietly but persistently. After weeks of peeking through the window, I entered the gallery to get a closer look. The owner saw me, smiled, but left me alone. I went back to visit the sculpture several times until one day the owner told me the story of the cross. When I got home, I could not get the cross out of my mind.

The next day I went back and purchased the cross for one of our chapels. The cross that at first I did not like now is one of my favorite pieces of art. In this case I did not fall in love with the art. Rather, I grew to love the art. Good art, divinely inspired art, has a way of getting to you. Sometimes, like in the unexpected encounter with *Milagros*, it happens in the blink of an eye. Sometimes, like in the persistent yet unexpected revelation of the Frederick Hart cross, it takes time. In both instances the impact is profound and lasting. In both instances the art accomplished its sometimes unexpected mission to give hope, enrich faith, and ultimately to draw us closer to God. That is why good art, divinely inspired art, is uniquely equipped to serve the liturgy and enrich our faith.

ART AS EVANGELIZATION

The Church has engaged the arts in many different ways throughout history, especially to assist with the spreading of the Gospel. This is one of the ways art has been and still is used as a tool of evangelization. Art was especially helpful during the Middles Ages, when most people were unable to read

Stained-glass window of Christ the King, The Basilica of Saint Mary, Minneapolis

or understand Latin. Many paintings, frescos, stained-glass windows, and sculptures depicted the story of the Bible and offered an alternative way for people to learn about our faith. These depictions were often described as the "Bible of the poor," because it was the only way that poor and uneducated people had access to Bible stories.

In addition to telling the story, the artists' visual interpretations added a layer of meaning to the Scripture stories for those who were able to read. Art enhances the meaning of the story because the images engage the viewer on a deeper level. Even nonfigurative art can impact the beholder through the use of color and shape. Warm colors, such as orange and red, along with curved lines, evoke happiness, while cold colors such as blue, gray and black—accompanied by square lines—can evoke sadness. Thus is the power of color, design, and art and their ability to express the sacred.

The art of music aiding the celebration, The Basilica of Saint Mary, Minneapolis

ART AND CELEBRATION

In addition to spreading the Good News, the Church is aware that art has the ability to enrich the celebration of the liturgy. Liturgy relies heavily on the arts, since its building is most often built to serve the celebration and is adorned with art to enhance the spiritual experience of the gathering. Music is composed to support every ritual act that is a part of the liturgy. And of course, the liturgical furnishings, objects, and vesture are designed and constructed specifically to support the liturgy. The arts provide décor for the celebration of the liturgy and inform everything that is necessary for the liturgy to be celebrated. It is hard to imagine how one could not be engaged with so much encouragement. And because we serve many cultures and ethnicities, the Church embraces many styles of art and welcomes many different cultural expressions in the service of the liturgy.

ART AND DEVOTIONS

Art has not only been used to support and enhance the communal celebration of the liturgy, but many private and public religious devotions also center on a work of art. The Stations of the Cross are a perfect example of art that serves our devotions. In order to celebrate this popular devotion, we need depictions of the different stations to behold. Stations can be figurative or abstract, elaborate or minimal, bronze cast or painted on wood, made in mosaics or sculpted in plaster. But in order for the Stations of the Cross to be celebrated, depictions of them are needed.

Other devotions also rely heavily on the arts. Statues are often the focal point of shrines dedicated to Jesus, Mary, and the saints. We surround our saints with candles. We dress them in regal garb or give them elaborate crowns. We carry them on our shoulders and process them through our cities. We touch their feet, their hands, or their head. We decorate them with flowers and wreaths and surround them with more flowers. None of these important aspects of our devotional life could happen if artists were not able to provide depictions of Jesus, Mary, and the saints. These depictions are constant reminders of what the saints have done for

Top: Jesus takes up his cross, the Second Station of the Cross
Bottom: Statues and candles invite us to devotional prayer

us and continue to do. They invite us into prayer with them for the needs of the world. And they encourage us to imitate them in our own lives so that we may become more like them.

ART IN OUR OWN IMAGE

I grew up with an image of Mary and Jesus in my room. Both had blond hair and blue eyes. This never struck me as odd until, in my later teenage years, I realized that Mary and Jesus must have had dark eyes and hair, since they were both Jewish and from the Middle East. Until then, I thought a blond and blue-eyed Jesus and Mary made perfect sense. I have come to learn that most people tend to visualize Jesus, Mary, and the saints in a way that is typical for their own culture. This is known as the visual inculturation of religion. It means that the Christian narrative that is shared by all cultures is told in the visual image of the local culture. If you look at the medieval depiction of Mary in the Low Countries, including Belgium, you will see that Mary is sitting in surroundings reflective of the time and is wearing clothes from that same time frame. She has Flemish almond eyes and pale skin, as is typical for aristocrats. The same Mary painted in the Baroque period in Spain appears as a Spanish Baroque queen. Our Lady of Guadalupe is an Aztec princess, while Our Lady of La'Vang in Vietnam appeared as a Hue woman.

Although some of these depictions are historically inaccurate, they are important because they allow people of different cultures to identify

Top: Our Lady of Africa
Bottom: Our Lady of La'Vang, Vietnam

with Christianity beyond the culture that was first presented to them through foreign missionaries. By depicting Jesus in their own image, people in each culture express and reinforce their belief that Jesus shared their humanity and died for their salvation. Thus, inculturated images help Christians make Christianity their own. Similar ownership occurred with depictions of Mary. Her many appearances in cultures beyond her own helped the faithful of different countries understand more fully that she is not only the Jewish Mother of Jesus but the mother of each one of us. Thus, she remains Mary, the Mother of Jesus, while at the same time she is known as Our Lady of Africa, Our Lady of Guadalupe, Our Lady of La'Vang, and Our Lady to many others.

FAITHFUL REFLECTIONS

We receive information in many ways as we grow from a small child to an adult person. What are your first memories of learning about Jesus and the Gospel stories? Was it through a story, a book, a painting, or a stained-glass window in church? For some 2,000 years, the Church has engaged the arts in order to tell the story of our faith, to enhance our liturgical celebrations, and to promote our devotions. This is how the Church tells its stories of faith. Imagine how you might depict the Gospel in your home. What are ways to tell a story of faith without words? Think about what colors or shapes you associate with different experiences of prayer: silence, praise, lamentation, intercession. Now create a prayer without words.

✦ *How is art used to enhance the liturgies at your church? What would you like to see?*

✦ *What kinds of devotions are encouraged by the works of art in your church? How do these works help you pray?*

✦ *How can you incorporate art in your home to support your life of faith and prayer? What is a favorite religious image that might help you create a prayer space?*

CHAPTER FIVE

SYMBOLIC FURNISHINGS USED FOR THE LITURGY

Many of us decorate our homes by painting the walls in pleasing colors, hanging up art, and placing furniture carefully throughout the house. Each room seems to call for its own kind of furniture. Beds go in bedrooms, sofas find their way to the living room, and a large table becomes the centerpiece of the dining room. In each case, the furniture we select is based on what we intend to do in a specific room. We sleep in our bedroom, so we place the bed there. We eat in the dining room, so we make sure it contains a table and chairs. We appoint our churches in a similar way with furnishings that serve the liturgy that is celebrated in them.

Baptismal font, St. Mary's Cathedral, Sydney

THE ALTAR TABLE

Altar, Cathedral of St. Vincent
of Saragossa, Malo, France

One winter the sacredness of the altar became clear to me. The choir was rehearsing in our chapel, and all the choir members had come in wearing thick coats to guard against the cold weather. The altar in the chapel is located in the center, with chairs flanking either side of it, and the choir members had laid their coats on the chairs. At one point, I walked in to the rehearsal with our pastor, and to our horror we noticed that choir members had not only tossed their coats over the chairs but over the altar as well. The pastor marched up to the altar and wiped it clean of all the coats in one fell swoop. It was a dramatic reminder that the altar is not just a piece of furniture. It actually is a symbol of Christ, both during and outside the celebration of the Eucharist. That is exactly the lecture our choir members were then embarrassed to receive. Needless to say, the altar has not been used as a coat rack since then.

Most religions have altars. Some have built them on the tops of soaring mountain peaks, near the edge of dormant volcanoes, or on the banks of rushing rivers. They are found in temples, cathedrals, churches, and chapels. In most instances, they were built so some kind of offering or sacrifice could be performed on them. The offering may have consisted of pouring wine or oil, or the altar could have served as a place for a burnt offering of wheat and barley. It may have been the place where an animal was sacrificed and, in some instances, altars were even used for human sacrifice. The difference between

Left: Altar by sculptor M.J. Anderson, St. James Cathedral, Seattle
Right: St. Joseph Chapel, The Basilica of Saint Mary, Minneapolis

these altars and the Christian altar table is that the latter is not only a place where we celebrate the sacrifice of Jesus and his death for our salvation, it is also a place of gathering for the followers of Jesus.

Throughout our 2,000-plus-year history of Christianity, the altar has evolved from a low table where Christ and the disciples reclined at the time of the Last Supper to a movable table in early basilicas, to an ornate construction fixed to the back wall of the church where the priest would celebrate Mass far away from the people and sometimes unseen behind curtains. Since the Second Vatican Council, the altar is now placed closer to the assembly so that the faithful can truly gather around the altar at which the Mass is celebrated.

Christian altars are made of all sorts of materials. There are massive stone altars that emphasize the sacrificial character of the Eucharist. There are simple wooden altars that underscore the altar as a table around which Christians gather. Some altars incorporate both wood and stone to highlight both sacrifice and gathering. Although the Church does not offer specifics for the design of an altar, the *GIRM* holds that "the altar, on which is effected the Sacrifice of the Cross made present under sacramental signs, is also the table of the Lord to which the People of God is convoked to participate in the Mass, and it is also the center of the thanksgiving that is accomplished through the Eucharist" (*GIRM* 296).

Unlike other liturgical furnishings, the altar is also considered a symbol of Christ, because the Mass is celebrated on it. The ritual for the *Dedication of a Church and an Altar* states that "the Church's writers have seen in the altar a sign of Christ himself. This is the basis for the saying: 'the altar is Christ'" (*DCA* 4).

The ambo is a place from where the word of God is proclaimed. Unlike the altar, which is truly a symbol of Christ, the ambo is not. Rather, the Gospel book from which the word of God is proclaimed is a symbol of Christ and thus receives the respect it is due. Nevertheless, because

Left: Historic ambo, Notre Dame Cathedral, Riez, France
Right: Modern ambo, Santa Maria de la Paz day chapel, Santa Fe

the word of God is proclaimed from the ambo, it is considered a place of importance. Its prominence and design also enables the assembly to hear and see the lector while he or she is proclaiming. This eye contact is important because it allows the assembly to listen better and receive the word more fully. The location, design, and material of the ambo calls attention to the prominence of the proclamation of the word in the liturgy and allows it to function as a place of proclamation.

FONT

Although early Christians required only running water for the celebration of the sacrament of baptism, the container for baptismal water gained importance over the course of the centuries. What began as a simple statement, such as, "Look, here is water! What is to prevent me from being baptized" (Acts 8:36) uttered by the eunuch of the candace of Egypt in response to the

Covered font, Cathedral Basilica-St. Louis

Apostle Philip telling him of the wondrous resurrection of Jesus Christ has evolved to baptismal fonts that are architecturally complex and rich in symbolism.

While rivers were the preferred places for early Christian baptism, they were soon moved inside. At first, baptisms were done in Roman baths. Then, when Christianity became the official religion of the Roman Empire, they moved to buildings designed specifically to celebrate the sacrament. The first of the baptisteries were built in repurposed baths that allowed for flowing water to be used. Soon, however, the growing number of baptisms required the building of baptisteries with their own fonts.

Because water was the fundamental symbol for baptism, early fonts were large and deep to allow for immersion, since that was how most Christians were baptized. However, due to the decrease of adult baptism in favor of infant baptism, the fonts grew smaller and were no longer built into the ground. Rather, they were placed on pedestals to accommodate the baptism of infants more easily. As the way of baptizing changed from immersion to affusion, or the pouring of water, less water was needed. So the basin of the fonts became smaller as well. In addition, baptismal water was being stolen for use with witchcraft, so locked covers were placed atop fonts, and they were placed behind locked doors. In this succession of events, we can see how important it is to understand the purpose and value of a symbol. The fundamental symbol of water that began with baptism in the river Jordan was now relegated to a small basin with a locked cover placed on top of a pedestal and hidden behind a locked gate.

Since the Second Vatican Council's reinstitution of the Rites of Christian Initiation of

Ancient immersion font where Saint Ambrose baptized Saint Augustine, Milan, Italy, AD 387

Adults (RCIA) encouraged a return to immersion as the norm for baptism, a greater emphasis has again been placed on water, rather than on its container as the symbol for baptism. Since more water is desired, the font has also become more substantial. The baptismal fonts in many of today's churches have a larger basin that is no longer hidden in a side chapel but prominently placed at the entrance of the church to emphasize that baptism is the first sacrament we receive and the sacrament by which we enter the Church.

The shape of the font offers another layer of meaning for understanding the sacrament. Some fonts are octagonal (eight-sided) to remind us of the eighth day, the day of the resurrection. These fonts symbolize how the newly baptized or neophytes share in the resurrection of Christ through their baptism. Other fonts are hexagonal (six-sided), pointing to the sixth day, or Friday, when we commemorate the death of Jesus. These fonts, like cruciform fonts, symbolize that in order to rise with Christ, we need to die with him in the waters of baptism. In some cases an octagonal floor design around a hexagonal font suggests that the baptized die with Jesus in the font but rise with him on the eighth day as they step out of the font. There are also round fonts that offer a reference to the font as a womb through which baptized neophytes are born into the Church.

No matter the shape of the font, it is the water it holds that gives the font its ultimate meaning as the place where new Christians are made.

Top: Adult baptism by immersion
Right: Mosaic font by Helen McLean, Church of the Resurrection, Cleveland

THE CELEBRANT'S CHAIR:
BISHOP, PRIEST, AND DEACON

The role of the celebrant is to lead the community in prayer. His place in the assembly should therefore support that purpose. The chair where the celebrant sits should be located so he can easily lead the service. The chair's design should also befit the leader of the community. At the same time, the chair is not to be confused with a throne, since the priest is the servant leader of the community, and his seat should reflect that humility.

The celebrant's chair is only to be used by ordained ministers. Even when a lay leader is celebrating in the absence of a priest, he or she may not use this chair. Lay leaders are to sit with the assembly and come forward to face the assembly at appointed times during the liturgy when they lead the community in prayer. This practice not only emphasizes that the lay leader is called forth from the assembly, but the empty chair symbolizes the absence of an ordained minister.

In his own cathedral, a bishop has a special chair reserved for him. The word "cathedral" is actually derived from the Latin word *cathedra*, which means "chair." This chair symbolizes the bishop's office. The cathedral is

Cathedra, St. Peter's Cathedral,
Belleville, Illinois

therefore the church with the bishop's chair. Because of this, the time a diocese is without a bishop is known as *sede vacante*, or "empty chair," meaning there is no one to occupy the *cathedra*.

The custom of the *cathedra* goes back to Roman times when leaders of the empire would pronounce judgments and new rulings as they sat in the chair that symbolized their office. The office of the bishop used Roman customs when their ministry was developed, and so the *cathedra*, or bishop's chair, came to symbolize the office of the bishop.

Traditionally, the bishop's chair is designed to be a bit more substantial and more ornate than the celebrant's chair. It is often personalized for each successive bishop who serves and sits in the *cathedra* by adding the coat of arms of the current bishop.

Top left: Deacon and presider chair,
St. Clare Church, O'Fallon, Illinois
Top right: Cathedra, The Cathedral of Christ
the Light, Oakland, California
Bottom: Cathedra, the Chair of St. Augustine,
Canterbury Cathedral, Canterbury, England

FAITHFUL REFLECTIONS

What preparations do you make when you are planning a birthday dinner or a more formal meal for guests who are invited to your home? Often we think through where people will sit, what kind of dishes and glassware will be used, and if we have enough chairs for everyone who will arrive. While these preparations can become an event in and of themselves, there is usually a greater meaning for the gathering that exceeds the practical yet purposeful needs at hand. Sometimes there is even a special plate for the main course or a special chair for the birthday boy or girl. Liturgical furnishings serve a similar, if not elevated, double role. First, liturgical furnishings serve the liturgy in a practical way. The priest needs a chair to sit in, and we need a place to put the bread and wine. But the furnishings also have a deeply symbolic meaning. The altar is a place of sacrifice and communion for all who gather. The chair is the place of presidency. Imagine what an altar and a chair might look like that holds this meaning. Now think about your own church or a church you might dream of building.

✦ *What does your church's altar and ambo look like? What shape do they share? What material are they made of?*

✦ *Can you see and touch the water in your church's baptismal font? What can you learn about baptism by looking at your font?*

✦ *Where is the celebrant's chair located? How does it support the role of a leader of the community?*

CHAPTER SIX

SYMBOLIC OBJECTS
USED FOR THE LITURGY

Every year a group of parishioners at The Basilica of Saint Mary in Minneapolis prepares an Easter fire that will be blessed during the Great Easter Vigil later that day, Holy Saturday. They place a twelve-foot cauldron in the center of the courtyard area in front of the basilica, and they fill it with wood. As dusk falls, they light the fire as parishioners start to gather around. The first to arrive are the elect who will be initiated into the Church that night. They stand closest to the fire with eager excitement. Slowly, the entire area fills with people looking forward to celebrating the resurrection of the Lord.

Every year the church requests a fire permit from the city and advises the fire department that an Easter fire will be lit, because inevitably someone will call and tell them that The

Basilica is on fire. A highway runs nearby and traffic slows whenever something happens on the plaza in front of The Basilica as people crane their necks to get a glimpse of what's going on. Thus is the power of the presymbolic human experience of fire and the power of liturgical symbols, such as the Easter fire. Good symbols, worthy liturgical objects, make an impact—like the Easter fire.

CROSS AND CRUCIFIX

Processional cross by Debra Korluka

The most recognized symbol of Christianity is the cross or crucifix. The difference between the two is that the crucifix is a cross with an image of the dead body of Jesus, or *corpus*, nailed to the cross. Though both the cross and crucifix are now almost commonplace and found in many shapes, sizes, and materials, it has not always been that way. The early Christians did not depict the cross at all but used other symbols, such as a Christ monogram or the fish. The first known depiction of the cross in reference to Christianity is a sarcastic rendition of a donkey on a cross with the inscription "Alexamenos worships his God." Clearly, the person who created this image intended to ridicule Alexamenos and his religion.

At least a century later—in the fourth century—Christians started displaying crosses and, more importantly, crucifixes. In these early versions, Jesus stands with both feet nailed to the cross. His eyes are open and there is no sign of suffering. He is clearly in control of his situation.

Gradually crucifixes came to show a suffering Jesus on the cross. By the tenth century his body began to sag and show signs of human suffering. After that point, two nails rather than one nail were pounded through both feet, which were placed on top of one another. By the fourteenth and fifteenth centuries, the body of Jesus began to be depicted with the many wounds he suffered during his repeated whipping.

Today we see crucifixes that emphasize the suffering of Jesus, as well as those that point to the resurrection. Some crucifixes even bear the risen Christ. The cross was the sign of ultimate humiliation in the Roman world, so it took some time for Christians to embrace this instrument of torture that became our pathway to salvation.

EASTER, OR PASCHAL, CANDLE

Who does not like to light candles? I always delight when parents bring their children to light votive candles. They carefully light a candle and place it in its holder, then stare at it for such a long time that I wonder what they are thinking. Light plays an important role in many religions. It often symbolizes the victory of good over evil, where evil is symbolized by darkness and good is symbolized by light. Light also adds ambiance or sets the mood of a gathering. The more important the dinner party, the more candles, and the taller the candelabras or candlesticks we display. This also holds true for the liturgy. At the most important of all liturgies, the celebration of the Easter Vigil, we use the most beautiful and the tallest candle of them all—the Easter candle.

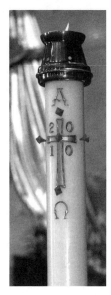

Every year, at the beginning of the Easter Vigil on Holy Saturday, a new Easter candle—known as the paschal, or Christ candle—is lit from the Easter fire and then blessed. The blessing consists of two prayers and a number of accompanying liturgical actions. The first prayer reads, "Christ, yesterday and today, the Beginning and the End, the Alpha and the Omega, all time belongs to him and all the ages; to him be glory and power through every age and for ever. Amen." As the priest prays this prayer, he carves a cross into the paschal candle, then the letters A and Ω, followed by the number of the current year of salvation. Today most Easter candles have the cross, the A and Ω, and the year already engraved or drawn on them so that the priest only signs them on the surface of the candle.

Blessing of the Easter Candle,
The Basilica of Saint Mary, Minneapolis

Afterward, the priest begins the second prayer, "By his holy and glorious wounds may Christ the Lord guard us and protect us. Amen." As he prays these words, he inserts five grains of incense into the candle that are often encased in wax-covered nails. These grains of incense and nails represent the five wounds of Christ in his hands, feet, and side.

Once the Easter candle is blessed, it is lit from the Easter fire and raised high, while the priest sings, "The Light of Christ." The people then respond, "Thanks be to God," and everyone lights his own candle from the Easter candle. This community lighting shows that all the baptized share in the light of Christ and are to be light to the world. The candle is then placed near the ambo, where it remains for the entire Easter season. As the liturgy continues, the paschal candle will be plunged three times into the baptismal water during the blessing of the water. This dunking symbolizes that Christ is fertilizing the baptismal womb from where new Christians will be born.

Outside of the Easter season, the Easter candle resides near the baptismal font. Baptismal candles are lit from the Easter candle during the celebration of baptisms throughout the entire liturgical year to symbolize that the newly baptized share in the resurrection of Christ. At funerals, the Easter candle is placed next to the coffin or the urn to symbolize Christ's resurrection and our participation in it through our baptism.

LITURGICAL BOOKS: *GOSPEL BOOK,* *LECTIONARY,* AND *SACRAMENTARY*

Among all the books that we use for the liturgy, the *Gospel Book* is the most important. This is because it contains the story of our faith as told by Matthew, Mark, Luke, and John. They are often known as "the evangelists." This refers to the fact that they evangelized or shared the story of Jesus Christ. The *Gospel Book* is the main symbol of Christ's presence because Christ, the Word of God, is contained in it, as told through the apostles.

The significance of the *Gospel Book* is shown when it is carried by the deacon or by the lector in the entrance procession of the liturgy. It is then carefully placed on the altar. During the Liturgy of the Word, the deacon or priest who is proclaiming the Gospel retrieves the *Gospel Book* from the altar and is flanked by candles and accompanied by incense as he processes it from the altar to the ambo, while everyone sings the Gospel acclamation. Upon arrival at the ambo, the *Gospel Book* is honored with incense and solemnly proclaimed by the deacon or priest. After the proclamation, the *Gospel Book* is honored with a kiss. When the bishop is present, the *Gospel Book* may be brought to him to venerate, and he may bless the people with the *Gospel Book*. Then the *Gospel Book* is set in a place of honor somewhere in the sanctuary.

Procession with the Gospel Book

The *Gospel Book* should be treated with respect at all times, since it is one of the main symbols of Christ's presence. The book itself should be one of substance to indicate the importance of the word of God in our church and in the liturgy. For centuries, the *Gospel Book* has been beautifully decorated and continues to be, with this understanding of Christ's presence in mind.

Some *Gospel Books* are decorated with a silver cover depicting Christ in the center, surrounded by the four evangelists. This image is known as the Tetramorph (see page 136). Sometimes the book cover pictures of Christ or the four evangelists on their own, or the cover is bound in beautiful leather and covered with a painted icon of Christ. There are many ways that the *Gospel Book* can witness the value of the word it contains.

In most churches, the *Gospel Book* is kept in the sacristy. However, some churches have created an area where the *Gospel Book* and other liturgical books, such as the *Sacramentary,* are enshrined when not used. This placement emphasizes the importance of these books. Other churches place the *Gospel Book* on a ledge on the front side of the ambo with it open to the Gospel of the day. Wherever it is placed, great care should be taken that the *Gospel Book* is stored in a respectful way, since it remains a symbol of Christ both during and outside of the celebration of liturgy.

In addition to the *Gospel Book*, the *Lectionary* is also used during Mass. This book contains all the liturgical readings for every day of the liturgical year. On Sunday, the *Lectionary* is used for the proclamation of the first and second reading and often for the psalm. During less solemn liturgies, such as a daily Mass, the Gospel may also be proclaimed from the *Lectionary.*

The *Sacramentary* is the third book used for the celebration of the Eucharist. This book contains all the prayers for the Mass and is used exclusively by the celebrant of the Mass to lead the assembly in prayer. It is not a symbol of Christ, so it is never carried in procession. Another name for the *Sacramentary* is the *Missal* or *Roman Missal.*

EASTER FIRE

Parishoners by the Easter fire before the Easter Vigil at The Basilica of Saint Mary, Minneapolis

Bonfires have been used during small family gatherings, as well as for large public celebrations, throughout history. In pre-Christian times, Europeans built big bonfires at the time of the solstice and equinox. Although the specific purpose of the fire is unknown, it is likely related to light and darkness and good and evil. Fires were lit to ward off evil, symbolized by darkness, while the fire symbolized light and goodness, as the light breaks through the darkness.

Christians adopted this symbolic way of warding off evil and darkness but gave it a Christian meaning. Thus the Easter fire is the Christian version of the spring equinox. For Christians, Jesus Christ is the Light of the World who broke through darkness once and for all. This is what we celebrate when we light the Easter fire.

There are also other fires in our tradition. The Christian version of the summer solstice fire is known as the Saint John's fire, since we celebrate the birth of Saint John the Baptist on June 24, about the time of the summer solstice. Saint John told us of the coming of the Savior, so as the light begins to fade after the longest day of the year, the Saint John's fire symbolizes the hope that six months later, on the shortest day of the year, at the beginning of the winter solstice, we will celebrate the birth of the Light of the World, Jesus Christ. The Christian version of the winter solstice bonfire is the custom of burning Christmas trees on Epiphany. In many countries, Christians bring their individual trees to a common place where all gather for a communal celebration of Epiphany that is marked by the lighting of the trees. Christmas lights and candles on trees also stem from the idea that light breaks through the darkness.

HOLY OILS

Ambry containing the holy oils,
St. Francis Cathedral, Santa Fe

Three kinds of blessed oil are used in the sacramental life of the Church: the oil of the catechumens, the oil for the anointing the sick, and the sacred chrism. Oils are blessed by the bishop during the chrism Mass that is traditionally celebrated on the morning of Holy Thursday to ready the new oils for the Easter Vigil. Today the chrism Mass is often celebrated earlier in Holy Week or even in the weeks leading up to Holy Week, to allow for greater attendance.

The oil of the catechumens is used when someone is preparing for two of the sacraments of initiation: baptism and confirmation. In the same way wrestlers use oil to prepare their bodies for the task at hand, catechumens are anointed with the oil of the catechumens so they might be spiritually prepared for their initiation and strengthened on their journey to the font. Infants who are baptized may also be anointed with the oil of the catechumens. However, this is optional. The custom of anointing children originated from adult initiation that was stretched over a longer period of time. Although infant baptism is a condensed version of adult initiation, children, too, need strength for their faith journey ahead, and their anointing with the oil of the catechumens accomplishes just that.

The oil of the sick is used for the sacrament of the anointing of the sick. This symbol clearly relies on the healing power inherent in oil. As oil soothes, smoothes, and salves the skin, we pray that it may do the same to the body, spirit, and soul of the sick person being anointed.

Sacred chrism is used during infant baptism, confirmation, the ordination of bishops and priests, and when dedicating a church or an altar. In all these cases, the oil symbolizes the imparting of the power of the Holy Spirit associated with the specific sacrament. As the oil permeates the skin, we pray that the Spirit penetrates the soul. "Chrism" is from a Greek verb meaning "to anoint." Sacred chrism is scented with perfume or balsam resin from trees so that the experience of being anointed is also an experience of smell.

The sacred oils are reserved in a container called an ambry that has traditionally been located either in the sanctuary or in the sacristy. In these cases, the ambry is often a metal box that has been recessed into the wall. The words, *Olea Sancta* or "Holy Oils" may be inscribed on the door, made out of solid metal with a lock. In newer churches, the ambry is located near the baptismal font and often incorporates glass so people can see the oils, rather than their being out of sight when they are encased in wood or metal.

CHALICE AND PATEN

Two of the most recognizable liturgical objects are the chalice and the paten that are used for the Liturgy of the Eucharist. The word "chalice" comes from the Latin word *calix* that in turn comes from the Greek word *kalus* and means "goblet."

From the early days of the Church, chalices were used as the drinking vessel of choice for the liturgy. They were first made of glass and pottery, but by the mid-fourth century they were often made of precious metals, richly decorated, and treated with great respect.

The oldest preserved examples of vessels used for the liturgy have larger bowls and two handles. The custom of drinking from a large shared cup during dinner was carried over into the liturgical gathering. The large bowl allowed for more wine to be used, and the two handles allowed for a better grip on the cup.

At some point after the fifth century, the practice of all those present sharing in the

Blood of Christ disappeared, and the priest became the only person receiving the Blood of Christ. Thus the bowl holding the wine became much smaller, since not as much wine was needed. The stem of the cup then became taller to make it easier to elevate the cup after the consecration. A knob in the middle of the stem was added to allow for a steadier holding of the chalice. The base also became broader to offer more stability to the top-heavy chalice.

Most every chalice also has a paten to accompany it. The chalice holds the wine, while the paten holds the host. They are often made of the same material, with related decorations, and the paten is shaped so that it can sit easily on the chalice. The practice of using a paten dates back to when the faithful rarely received Communion and the priest would consecrate only one host at Mass for his own communion. Today many hosts are consecrated at parish Sunday Masses, so individual patens are rarely used, and patens or plates for the hosts are much larger and no longer sit on top of the chalice.

When Communion under the form of both bread and wine is shared, there is often a principal chalice used by the priest and deacon, while several smaller cups are used for the distribution of the precious Blood to the assembly. Though we commune from different cups, the principal chalice symbolizes our unity in the Blood of Christ.

MONSTRANCE

A monstrance is an elaborately decorated object that is used to hold the consecrated host during exposition of the Blessed Sacrament, adoration, benediction, and processions with the Blessed Sacrament. The word "monstrance" comes from the Latin verb *monstrare,* meaning "to show." Originally a monstrance could be created to hold either a relic of a saint or the consecrated host. Today "monstrance" is exclusively used when referring to a vessel designed to hold the Blessed Sacrament. Similar vessels designed to hold relics of the saints are called "reliquaries."

Although the earliest monstrances differed in their design, today most are shaped in a similar way. The base is usually rather broad to assure stability. The stem is tall and has a knob in the middle to allow for easier handling. An aureole or sunburst is the main part of the monstrance and sits on the stem. In the middle of the aureole is the crystal container that holds and reveals the consecrated host. This container is known as the "gloria." The earliest monstrances did not have a gloria or crystal inset to hold the host because the need to see the host for veneration did not exist. A fully exposed host did not become the norm for adoration until after the Council of Trent in the mid-sixteenth century. When the host is displayed in the monstrance, it is first placed between two circular glass plates connected by precious metal that is known as the "luna." The luna keeps the host in place in the monstrance so it is secured with the reverence it is due.

The gloria is to be surrounded by rays of light made of precious metal, often gilded silver. Additional decorations are also permitted. As a result, many monstrances are completely made of precious metal, are richly decorated, and precious stones are sometimes imbedded in them.

CIBORIUM

A ciborium is made to hold the consecrated hosts that are used for the Communion of the faithful. Its shape is often similar to the chalice, although the cup is often wider so it can hold more hosts. Because a ciborium holds the body of Christ, it is made of precious metal, either gilded silver or gold. Ciboriums also have lids, because consecrated hosts that remain unconsumed after a given Mass are reserved in a ciborium and need to be stored properly. Some lids are dome-shaped to accommodate more hosts, and the top of the lid is often decorated with a cross or a small globe topped with a cross. In addition to the theological references, this adornment also allows for the easy removal of the lid.

In the past, a ciborium was covered with a special veil before it was placed in the tabernacle. Though no longer practiced in many churches, this veil consisted of a piece of cloth in the shape of a Greek cross, with the arms of the cross both the same length and with a small slit in the center. The cross on top of the monstrance cover was placed through the slit, thus allowing the four sides of the cross-shaped veil to cover the monstrance.

INCENSE AND THURIBLE

The use of incense in the liturgy can be traced to ancient Jewish temple rituals and imperial court rituals. "Incense" comes from the Latin verb *incendere*, meaning "to burn." In the Christian liturgy, incense is placed on burning coals to release both smoke and aroma. It is thus a symbol that we encounter visually as well as with our sense of smell.

The purpose of incense in the liturgy embraces offering, honoring, and imploring. In the same way as incense was burnt as an offering to God in the Old Testament, we, too, burn incense during the liturgy as a visual reference of the prayers we offer. "Let my prayer be counted as incense before you, and the lifting up of my hands as an evening sacrifice" (Psalm 141:2).

We also use incense as a sign of honoring during the liturgy when we incense all symbols of Christ, including the altar, the *Gospel Book*, the eucharistic elements, the priest, the people of God, the cross, and the Easter candle. When we honor these people and things with incense, we honor Christ.

In the Catholic Church, incense is burned in a thurible. The word "thurible" comes to us via the Latin *thuribulum,* which shares a root with the Greek verb *thuein,* meaning "to sacrifice." The basic shape of the thurible is a metal bowl with enough

room for at least one coal and a perforated cover that allows the incense to bellow out through its holes. At least one chain, if not several, are used to hold the bowl and the cover together and to allow for the swinging of the thurible. An incense boat, whose purpose is to hold the incense that will be placed on the coals during the liturgy, is usually made to match the thurible. Incense is carried by a thurifer, the bearer of the thurible, at the beginning of solemn processions.

HOLY WATER STOOPS AND FOUNTS

When I was growing up, my siblings and I all had a small holy water stoop or ornate cup-like container attached to the wall next to the door frame of our bedrooms. We received these containers as a gift at our baptism or first Communion. The first thing we did when entering our rooms was to dip our finger into the holy water and bless ourselves. Then we would pray, and only after that would we be allowed to go to bed. The custom of a holy water stoop outside a bedroom is rare today and rarer is the custom to bless

Sprinkling rite during the Easter Vigil

ourselves when entering a bedroom before going to sleep. This act of blessing ourselves at church, as well as the sprinkling rite at the beginning of the Mass, share one meaning, which is to remind ourselves of our baptism and the rights and responsibilities that come with that declaration. The sacrament of baptism is known as the sacrament that offers us entrance into the Church, the body of Christ, and the Christian community. It is the first sacrament, and without it, no other sacrament can be celebrated. If baptism is the source of all other sacraments, then it makes sense to refer to baptism whenever another sacrament is celebrated, be that verbally or symbolically. At certain times the liturgy makes this connection explicitly, such as at the beginning of a funeral Mass, when the body of the deceased is sprinkled with holy water in remembrance of the deceased's baptism. At other times the connection is less explicit, like when we are invited to bless ourselves with holy water whenever we enter a church.

What better place to go to remind ourselves of our baptism than the baptismal font. New and remodeled churches have large baptismal fonts at the entrance of the church. Their size and location alone make it clear that baptism is indeed the first sacrament. In these churches, the font also functions as the place where people go to bless themselves upon entering the church. This action of blessing is not new; there is, however, a new location for the action. Previous to the Second Vatican Council, baptismal fonts were hidden in baptismal chapels where locked doors made it impossible for the font to be used outside of baptisms. Thus small holy water founts or stoops were located, in *lieu* of the font, at every door of the church, so that the faithful would have easy access to holy water. These small hand founts are not seen as often today, since many churches favor the fuller symbol of the baptismal font.

FAITHFUL REFLECTIONS

There are many liturgical symbols that are used for the celebration of our sacraments. We might recognize them by sight, but we might not know their name or even what they are used for, where they are from, or what they might mean. The next time you go to church, look around—really look around—and think about what you see that is used to celebrate the sacraments. There may be several objects or furnishings. Look at them carefully and take some time to think about them and meditate on them. What do they look like? What do they express? What do they tell you?

✦ *What sacred dishes do you have at home? How can the plates and bowls you eat on at home help make every meal one to recall Christ's sacred presence and give thanks?*

✦ *What symbols do you use in your home that you see at church? What symbols of faith can you bring into your home to make your prayer more meaningful?*

✦ *How is incense used to honor Christ's presence in your church? What are other ways to honor Christ's presence? How can you honor Christ's presence in your home, in your work, and with friends in your daily living?*

CHAPTER SEVEN

SYMBOLIC CLOTHING USED FOR THE LITURGY

A friend from New York told me about a woman who would beg for money each day while he was having lunch in a park. Although she said nothing, she would walk by and extend her hand toward him, then wait for him to give her money. The woman stood out from others in the park because she was wearing a nun's habit, including a wimple covering her neck and head. After several weeks, my friend finally told her it was rude to impersonate a nun in order to get money. Without missing a beat she replied, "I never told you I was a nun!" And in truth she had not, at least not in so many words. However, the clothing she wore told him otherwise, and it is hard to imagine that she didn't want people to think she was a nun.

First Communion, The Basilica of Saint Mary, Minneapolis

A server wearing a cassock and surplice

Certain types of clothing tell a story or imply a profession. When we see someone wearing scrubs, we associate her with a hospital setting. If someone is wearing a clerical collar, we presume he is a priest or a minister. A person who wears a chasuble is automatically connected with the liturgy. Clothing has a symbolic character that helps people make clear associations between dress and role.

The Roman Catholic Church has a long tradition of liturgical vestments, most of which have their origin in the daily dress of the Roman Empire. Although the specifics of who can wear what for which services is clear today, liturgical garb was ruled for centuries by local custom. It was not until the thirteenth century that Church law began to regulate what could be worn at Mass. Our current *Code of Canon Law* also devotes several paragraphs to liturgical vesture.

The purpose of wearing special garb for the celebration of the liturgy is twofold. First, it allows the congregation to differentiate between the different ministers, since laypersons, deacons, priests, and bishops all wear different dress. Second, vestments add solemnity to the celebration and indicate what liturgical season and what type of liturgy is being celebrated, since vestments differ for various liturgical seasons and celebrations.

Vestments are distinguished from one another by their shape, their color, and sometimes by the decorations that are applied to the vestments. The colors used for vestments follow the colors of the liturgical year. Purple is used for the penitential and preparatory seasons of Advent and Lent, white is used for the seasons of Christmas, Easter, and for other particular feasts; green is used for Ordinary Time; and red is used on Palm Sunday, Good Friday, Pentecost, and on the feast days of martyrs. Vestment colors may also relate to the sacrament that is celebrated, regardless of the liturgical season. White is worn for weddings and funerals, although the former color for funerals, black, is still allowed in certain dioceses. Red may be worn at confirmations. Though the symbolic meaning of vestments is primarily drawn from their form, shape, and color, sometimes other symbols are added onto a vestment to enhance their connection with a particular feast or season. These details always need to be approached with care so that any images that are added to vesture do not diffuse the main symbol, which is the garment itself.

A server wearing an alb

ALB

The most common and basic of all liturgical vesture is the alb, a white garment that stretches to the ankle. "Alb" is derived from the Latin word *albis*, which means "white." This is the one vesture that may be worn by ordained and lay ministers alike, because it is the baptismal garment that may be worn by all the baptized and does not denote a ministry in the Church.

The origin of the alb is found in the simple Roman tunic. Like all liturgical vesture, it has been made of various materials with many decorative elements throughout its history. Today's albs are usually simple in style and material, although some churches use more traditional albs that are trimmed with lace at the bottom and around the sleeves.

Some parishes also use hooded albs that are traditionally reserved for monks. The white hood is used to cover the black or brown hood that is part of a monk's habit, a garment worn by all monks.

An alb is the foundational liturgical garment that is worn beneath any other garments that ordained ministers wear. If an ordained minister wears a cassock, or another form of clerical garb, then an alb is worn over it.

A shorter variant on the alb is the surplice. This is the white garment worn over the cassock by some altar boys and by clergy for certain liturgies.

A deacon wearing his stole

STOLE

A stole is a band of colored textile, often silk or wool, that is worn by ordained ministers. "Stole" comes from the Latin *stola,* which means "garment." During Roman times, the *stola* served as a kind of wide scarf that was worn by men and women alike and wrapped generously around their shoulders. Gradually the *stola* worn by men during liturgy became narrow and came to be seen to reference a certain office, rather than a garment intended to offer warmth. As stoles became more narrow, they also became more decorative.

Today there are two different kinds of stoles, one style for deacons and another for a priest. The stole worn by a deacon is worn over the left shoulder, while wearing an alb, and is covered by a dalmatic or cope. A priest wears the stole around his neck, over the alb, and under the chasuble or cope when they are worn.

DALMATIC

The dalmatic is a vestment deacons wear during the celebration of the Eucharist or other appropriate liturgical functions. It is worn over the alb and stole. Like all liturgical garb, it has its origin in the Roman Empire, where it was worn as a form of secular clothing. By the fourth century, however, the dalmatic was firmly established as a liturgical vestment.

The dalmatic is a simple square tunic with wide sleeves. Today the sides are usually sewn together, but examples still exist of dalmatics that are open on the sides, similar to the scapular garment worn by men and women in monastic religious communities.

The color of the dalmatic depends on the liturgical season and feast. Some dalmatics are also adorned with additional symbols or decorative elements that refer to the sacraments celebrated by the deacon wearing them.

Top: A deacon with the Gospel Book, *wearing a dalmatic*
Right: Full view of a dalmatic

CHASUBLE

A priest wearing a chasuble

The chasuble is worn by priests and bishops for the celebration of the Eucharist. This vestment also has its origins in a Roman secular garment that was most often worn for traveling. It was appropriately named *casula*, a word that means "little house," illustrating the fact that a chasuble covers almost the entire person. The first type of *casula* featured large circular pieces of cloth with a hole in the center. It was pulled over the head, like an oversized poncho, and reached nearly to the ground. The *casula* needed to be gathered up at the arms in order to reveal hands and arms.

As the use of the chasuble became more popular in the liturgy, it was adapted to the specific needs of the Mass. Thus the sides were made shorter to free up the hands, resulting in what looked more like an oversized bib rather than a poncho, and certainly not a *casula*. The sides became even shorter and disappeared altogether in the sixteenth century to allow for a priest to easily elevate the Eucharist over his head, since he was celebrating the Mass with his back to the people, who needed to be able to view the consecrated Eucharist after the consecration. This type of chasuble is known as the "fiddle back" because it is shaped like a violin. Today's chasubles resemble the original shape of the *casula* more closely and are made of more ample material.

Like dalmatics, chasubles follow the colors of the liturgical feasts and seasons. They are often made out of wool, silk, or other natural materials. Although chasubles throughout history have been heavily decorated with symbols, or abstract or decorative designs, today's chasubles rely on color and fabric to suggest the liturgical days and year and are much simpler in their expression.

COPE

Bishops, priests, and deacons wear a cope for liturgical celebrations other than the celebration of the Eucharist. "Cope" is rooted in the Latin word *cappa,* meaning "cape." Not surprisingly, the cope is a large mantle that is open in front, held together by a clasp, and reaches to the ground.

Except for the elimination of a hood that offered protection from the sun and rain, the cope has not changed much in shape since its earliest liturgical use as far back as the sixth century. At that time, the hood had a practical purpose, which was

A priest wearing a stole and cope

to protect its wearer from the elements during outdoor processions. Gradually the hood became an ornamental element and shifted into the back panel, as is seen on many copes from the Middle Ages. This panel is often richly embroidered with Christian symbols or images of saints and decorated with fringes and a tassel.

Today's copes are much simpler than their medieval counterparts and usually do not include the back panel or symbolic decorative elements.

Antique cope with the Sacred Heart embroidered on the panel

HUMERAL VEIL

The humeral veil is worn only during benediction with the Blessed Sacrament and during processions with the Blessed Sacrament. It is a long rectangular piece of cloth used by the ordained minister to hold the monstrance or the ciborium.

The humeral veil or shoulder veil is usually about eight feet long and one and a half feet wide. Pockets are sewn into the inside of each side of the veil to enable the user to more easily hold the monstrance or ciborium. The origin of this veil goes back to the Roman imperial custom of servants being ready with a similar veil, known as the *sudarium*, to hold whatever object might be handed to them. This practice infers that the servant is not worthy to touch the object directly.

Since during processions with the Blessed Sacrament or during benediction the ordained minister holds the vessel containing the Body of Christ, the wearing of the humeral veil emphasizes the sacredness of the Blessed Sacrament being carried or raised.

MITER

The miter is the pointed hat worn by bishops and abbots during certain parts of the celebration of the liturgy. The word is derived from the Greek *mitra*, which means "headband." Its origin seems to have been the headdress worn by officials in the Roman imperial court. Those early miters were different than today's miters.

The first references to the current shape of the miter are found about the year 1000. It consists of two pointed panels sewn together with two cloth flaps in the back. Since 1200, bishops have commonly worn this type of miter.

During the course of history, abbesses—the women leaders of certain ancient abbeys—had the right to wear miters, although they were shaped differently and mostly were carried behind the abbess rather than worn by her in processions. Some medieval depictions of the foundresses of these abbeys show them with the same miters as worn by bishops.

CROSIER

The crosier or pastoral staff carried by bishops, abbots, and at times by abbesses is one of the emblems of the office of the bishop, the abbot, or the abbess. It is inspired by the shepherd's custom of carrying a crook when shepherding his flock and symbolizes the principal role of the bishop, abbot, or abbess as shepherds of their communities.

The crosier can be made out of any material, ranging from wood to precious metal. It is carried in procession and held during particular liturgical acts, such as preaching or confirmation. However, bishops can only use the crosier within their diocese, and abbots and abbesses within their abbeys, unless they are otherwise given permission by local Church authorities.

PECTORAL CROSS

Many people practice the custom of wearing a small cross around their neck. They might wear it as one would a decorative necklace to testify to their faith, or inside their shirt as a form of protection. A pectoral cross, however, is much larger and only worn by certain people to show their ecclesiastical rank in Church leadership. As a result, the pectoral cross is most often worn by bishops, abbots, and abbesses.

Pectoral cross with image of the victorious lamb, Treasury of St. Mary's Cathedral, Sydney

The name for pectoral cross comes from the Latin word *pectoralis*, meaning "chest." Not surprisingly, the pectoral cross is worn hanging from a chain or rope over the heart or the chest. It is usually made of precious metals and adorned with precious or semiprecious stones. During the liturgy, the pectoral cross is worn above the bishop's vestments and hangs from a green and white braided rope with a tassel on the back. A cardinal's colors for this braided rope are gold and red.

A bishop with miter, crosier, and pectoral cross

RING

When he is consecrated, a bishop receives a ring, in addition to other symbolic objects, such as the miter and the crosier. The origin of the bishop's ring might lie in the fact that documents in early Christianity were sealed with the ring of the holder of the office that issued the document. The seal validated the document.

Although bishops no longer validate documents with their ring, the ring retains its symbolic meaning, showing the supreme loyalty of the bishop to Christ and his Church, similar to the union expressed by a wedding ring.

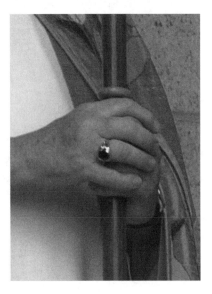

PALLIUM

A pallium is worn by the pope and a metropolitan archbishop who presides over a number of surrounding dioceses. The word is derived from the Latin *palla*, meaning woolen cloak. Today the pallium is a three-inch-wide white band made of lamb's wool. It is worn over the chasuble during the celebration of the Mass and has a lappet or tail-like piece of cloth on the front and the back. The pallium is decorated with five crosses that reference the five wounds of Christ and three pins to symbolize the nails with which Christ was nailed to the cross.

The pallium is woven by nuns at the Saint Agnes convent in Rome. The wool is from carefully selected lambs that are raised by the Cistercian monks at Rome's Tre Fontane Abbey. New metropolitan archbishops receive their pallium from the pope on the feast of Saints Peter and Paul (June 29) to show that they are the pope's representatives in their metropolitan areas.

PEOPLE'S DRESS

Although most people have become rather informal when it comes to their selection of clothes, they still opt to wear certain types of garb to certain types of events. People wear different clothes to a baseball game than to a picnic, even though both are casual events. Likewise, varying degrees of formal dress are seen when attending a fine dinner or church. Clothes not only dress the body but communicate messages, whether the person wearing them intends to do so or not. Importantly, dress often communicates how wearers feel about the event they attend.

Although dress is a personal matter, there is appropriate and inappropriate dress for worship. Since no one wants to hear that his or her outfit is inappropriate for church, some good questions to ask before leaving for church are: "Do my clothes speak to the importance of the celebration of the Eucharist?" If not, then it is best to wear something else; or, "Will what I am wearing distract others from their prayer and worship?" If so, then it is best to wear something else. All that is associated with the liturgy underlines the importance of the celebration and supports the celebration at hand. This includes our attire.

FAITHFUL REFLECTIONS

Perhaps the most important piece of clothing we own is our baptismal gown. No, not the one you were baptized in when you were a small child, but the one we each wear today. Our actions, attitudes, and manner of presentation all speak loudly about how we view our baptism and Christian commitment to act as Jesus would at all times. As Christians, we always have the opportunity to serve as a witness to the love and care of God. The wearing of special clothing as a minister at Sunday Mass—whether as a deacon, priest, or newly baptized—is a wonderful way to witness God's presence. However, our hearts can also express the jewels of our faith as they spill out in respect for all those around. Look closely at the vestments at your church. What do you notice? The liturgy supports and serves the building-up of the kingdom of God. All that we express symbolically, including vesture and all the accents of jewelry and tassels, are to do the same. You may have heard the expression, "wearing your heart on your sleeve." This is how Christians are to witness at all times. What are you wearing today?

✦ *What type of clothing do you feel most comfortable wearing? What makes the difference for you?*

✦ *What events compel you to think with care about what you are wearing? What clothing fully expresses your faith?*

✦ *What vesture do you often see at your church, and what does it signify? What don't you see?*

CHAPTER EIGHT

SYMBOLIC GESTURES IN THE LITURGY

When my great-grandfather died, wakes were still held at home, where funeral directors would turn living rooms into a funeral chapel by draping the walls and windows with black curtains. I remember large candelabras flanking my great-grandfather's body and the entire house filled with dark quiet.

On the day of the funeral, pallbearers carried my great-grandfather's casket to the horse-drawn hearse, and we walked from the house to the church. After the service, we walked to the cemetery in a procession led by servers with a cross and candles, followed by priests dressed in surplices and black stoles. We walked behind the hearse accompanied by the sound of the death toll and passersby who would stop for a

Advent procession, The Basilica of Saint Mary, Minneapolis

moment and remove their hats while facing the funeral procession. We then went to an open tomb, and at the end of a brief service, the coffin was lowered into the tomb, and all of us threw handfuls of dirt on the coffin as we filed by.

Everyone was dressed in black, and the women wore black veils. Our immediate family wore black for six months, and then we were allowed to wear gray and dark blue for the six months following. It was only after we had marked the one-year anniversary of my great-grandfather's death with a memorial Mass that we were allowed to again wear other colors. My great-grandmother wore black until her death.

Much has changed since that time. Today the custom of wearing black for great lengths of time after the loss of a loved one has completely disappeared. Family members go to the cemetery but rarely wait for the coffin to be lowered into the ground before they leave. Some cemeteries advise people to say their last goodbye in a specially constructed chapel on the grounds rather than going to the graveside. Only after everyone has left is the coffin brought to the burial plot and lowered into the ground. Such gestures as waking the body in the home, processing to the church and finally to the cemetery, throwing soil on the coffin, and wearing distinctive clothing have all disappeared in favor of new customs that often hide the reality of death as much as possible. While well-intended, the disappearance of these rituals and customs deprives us of rituals and symbolic actions that help us grieve.

Gestures such as processing behind the hearse, wearing particular clothing, and throwing dirt all help us express our deepest feeling of loss. Our ritual and liturgies are also packed with gestures that help us celebrate moments of great joy or mark important transitions in our lives. We submerge one another in water, we anoint with oil, we gather around the Easter fire, we wash feet and sometimes kiss them, we break bread and share it with one another, we drink from one cup, we receive ashes at the beginning of Lent, we burn incense, we light candles, we kneel and prostrate on the ground, we hug, we touch, we kiss the *Gospel Book*, the cross, the altar, and sometimes one

another. We are the BODY of Christ, and our liturgy celebrates the physicality of this body of Christ. We celebrate with word, through symbols, and in gestures.

About symbolic postures to be used for the Eucharist, the *GIRM* states: "A common bodily posture, to be observed by all those taking part, is a sign of the unity of the members of the Christian community gathered together for the Sacred Liturgy" (*GIRM* 42). It is important, then, for the whole body to know these liturgical gestures so we can do them together.

Cameroon Gospel procession, Minneapolis

PROCESSIONS

In certain parts of the world, grand processions mark Holy Week, and *Corpus Christi* processions are still commonplace. Today, while there is a resurgence of these in the United States, most of us are familiar with more modest practices, such as the entrance procession at the beginning of Mass, the Gospel procession, the procession with the gifts, the Communion procession, and the closing procession.

Processions serve the practical purpose of moving a group of people, who are often carrying something, such as the Eucharist or the *Gospel Book*, from one place to another. More importantly, they also hold a symbolic meaning. If we think about the solemn entrance at festive Masses, it would be much more efficient to have the priest walk from the sacristy to the sanctuary in a direct line. But when we add different people to the procession, we take a somewhat circuitous route. Thus, in addition to transporting people and objects from one place to the next, processions become symbolic walks of our journey of faith from baptism to burial. It is a walk that echoes our pilgrim path here on earth: one that holds its own twists and turns, but one that we will never walk alone.

On some occasions, everyone participates in liturgical processions, such as in the procession on Palm Sunday of our Lord's passion when everyone joins the commemorative procession of Jesus' entrance into Jerusalem. The whole community also participates in the Easter Vigil procession as we walk from the fire outside into the church, holding candles lit from the newly lighted paschal candle. Most often, however, only a representative group joins in the procession. And yet, even though we may not be able to physically participate, the procession represents each one of us, and all of us participate spiritually.

Some processions are highly orchestrated, such as Gospel processions and opening processions on high holy days, such as Christmas and Easter. There are also more informal processions, such as the gathering "procession" that brings us all to church from our individual homes. This grand procession starts as a number of smaller processions that meet in the church parking lot and culminate in the entrance procession. At the end of Mass, we see the grand opening procession reverse as the formal liturgical procession processes out, followed by the assembly, who then split into numerous smaller processions as people go to their cars and back to their daily lives.

Aztec Dancers on the feast of Our Lady of Guadalupe, Minneapolis

GENUFLECTING

Upon entering a church, there are actions we traditionally perform. First, we make our way past the baptismal font, where we bless and remind ourselves of our baptismal rights and obligations. Then we go into the main body of the church proper, where we genuflect as a sign of reverence toward the Blessed Sacrament, reserved in the tabernacle. If the Blessed Sacrament is reserved in a separate chapel, we make a profound bow toward the altar, since the altar is a symbol of Christ. Both actions are threshold gestures of entrance that assist us in making the transition from the secular world to the sacred ground of the liturgy.

We also genuflect every time we pass before the Blessed Sacrament, whether it is reserved in the tabernacle or exposed in the monstrance. We do this out of reverence for the Real Presence of Christ in the Blessed Sacrament. During the celebration of the liturgy, we genuflect when we enter and leave the sanctuary if the tabernacle is located in the sanctuary. The practice of genuflecting on both knees when the Blessed Sacrament is exposed is no longer customary, but a single genuflection is always an appropriate expression of reverence.

SIGNING WITH THE SIGN OF THE CROSS

There are two moments in the Mass when we sign ourselves with the sign of the cross: the beginning and the end. After the opening procession, the celebrant leads us in the sign of the cross. This is our mark. It sets us apart as Christians. Every time we gather, we do so "in the name of the Father, the Son and the Holy Spirit," and we make the sign of the cross.

During the Liturgy of the Word, we sign ourselves when the priest announces the Gospel, saying, "A reading from the Holy Gospel according to...." We respond by saying, "Glory to you, O Lord," while at the same time marking our forehead, lips, and heart with the sign of the cross. This gesture indicates our desire and hope that the word of God we are about to hear may be in our mind, on our lips, and in our heart, so that we may be inspired by the word, willing to testify to the word, and moved to live it, as we carry the word in our heart.

The cross is our sign because it is by the cross that we have been saved. The cross is the instrument of our salvation. At the end of Mass, the celebrant sends us into the world to live as the body of Christ. Before we leave, he calls down God's blessing upon us as he signs us with the sign of our salvation to give us strength for our journey of faith and all we encounter beyond the doors of the church.

ORANS

The term "orans" comes from the Latin verb *orare*, which means "to pray." Orans refers to a specific prayer posture where both hands are extended upward in prayer. The gesture predates Christianity and is currently used in various religions. It seems a natural gesture to use when we ask someone for something or plead with another human being. Thus it is a compelling gesture to use when seeking God's care.

An early Christian painting of Noah in the gesture of orans

The oldest images of Christians depicted in the orans position are found on tombs in the catacombs, an ancient, complex system of tunnels used to bury early Christians. In hundreds of instances, a woman is portrayed standing with her hands raised up to heaven in prayer. These women are believed to represent the soul of the deceased pleading for mercy, whether they are male or female. Early depictions of Mary and the saints are also shown in the orans position as they plead for God's mercy in prayer.

The priest at Mass uses the orans gesture when he prays to God on behalf of the people. This includes the opening and closing prayer of the Mass, the prayer over the gifts, the Eucharistic Prayer and the Lord's Prayer.

Many assemblies have developed a custom of joining the priest's gesture as they, too, extend their hands in the orans position during the Lord's Prayer. This is neither suggested nor forbidden in the rubrics that guide the details of the celebration of the Eucharist, although it can be seen as quite a symbol of unity when all people extend their hands in the same position while praying the same prayer. People also hold hands in an attempt to show this unity. Again, there are no rubrics for or against this gesture; however the ancient gesture, practiced over several centuries, even before Christ, seems more appropriate than a newer expression that holds less meaning.

PRIEST WASHES HIS HANDS

Many religions perform ablutions or washings with water as part of their ritual and prayer. This may include a ritual washing of feet, hands, and face—or even of the whole body. There are two components of ritual washing. One is practical, and the other is symbolic. On a purely practical level, washing is intended to simply clean the worshiper's face, hands, feet, or body. The symbolic meaning of washing varies from ritual to ritual and from religion to religion.

Ritual washings have been part of the Christian tradition from its inception. The ritual bath that is part of the sacrament of baptism is the most dramatic in its execution as well as in content, because it symbolizes our entrance into the body of Christ and the beginning of our life as a Christian. The other ablutions in the Catholic ritual tradition are more ritualistic and do not cause sacramental change in the person who experiences them as much as they do in the sacrament of baptism. Nevertheless, these other ablutions, including the washing of the hands by the priest during Mass, are significant.

While highly symbolic today, the origin of the *lavabo,* or "the washing of the hands" by the priest, was practical in its beginnings, due to the nature of the offertory procession. In earlier times, people literally brought the work of their hands: vegetables, chickens, and other gifts to offer to God for the well-being of the community. After receiving these fruits of the earth, the priest would incense them. This, too, was quite involved, so collectively receiving the gifts and incensing them resulted in the real need for the priest to wash his hands before continuing on with the Mass.

Today the procession of the gifts is more formal and consists mostly of monetary gifts, bread, and wine. Incensing, too, has become more contained and does not require the same type of cleanup as in days past. Thus the washing of the hands, once a practical act, became a symbolic act as its meaning and the need for washing shifted from the cleansing of actual dirt to the cleansing of spiritual dirt. This understanding is expressed when, while washing his hands, the priest now prays, "Wash me, O Lord, from my iniquity and cleanse me from my sin."

The practical aspect of the lavabo has now come full circle as a heightened concern for hygiene has resulted in this gesture of handwashing before distributing Communion again holds both a practical and symbolic meaning.

THE SIGN OF PEACE

There is a wonderful icon image of Saint Peter and Saint Paul greeting one another with a holy kiss of peace. The icon portrays the original greeting of peace between Christians, that being a kiss. This type of greeting was common both inside and outside the liturgy.

Though this custom is ancient, the Church recognizes that some cultures might not want to kiss strangers, so other options have been provided: a hug of peace, a handshake of peace, or, in some Asian cultures, the traditional bow of peace. Each of these gestures involves different levels of touching, relative to how comfortable a particular culture is with physical contact. During the sign of peace in the United States, it is common to shake the hand of those we don't know well and to hug or kiss friends or family with whom we are more familiar. The simple action of sharing peace with one another has its foundation in Jesus Christ, the source of our lasting peace, the one who grants us peace, and the one who invites us into peace. As Christians who share in that peace, we are to share it with one another. Therefore, before we approach the table of the Lord at Communion, we affirm our unity in the peace of Christ by sharing a sign of peace with one another.

More important than the type of gesture is the understanding that this moment in the liturgy is to affirm the peace that comes from Christ and our participation in it, rather than an extended time to greet or visit with one another.

THE COMINGLING

The symbolic gesture of comingling was introduced into the liturgy for a specific theological reason. Though the gesture is still used today, it has lost its original meaning and has received a new theological interpretation.

The origins of comingling date back to the early Church. As early as the second century, bishops would send part of the eucharistic bread, known as *fermentum* or leaven, to nearby bishops. The bishop who received the *fermentum* would add it to the cup and consume it during the next Mass he celebrated. This is believed to have been done as a sign of unity among the bishops. The pope, too, sent out *fermentum* to the bishops as a sign of unity. The term *fermentum* may have been used because the Eucharist is understood to be the leaven of our Christian life, and we are to be leaven for the world.

As Christianity spread throughout the Roman Empire, particularly outside of cities into the countryside, it became necessary for the bishops to send some of their priests into the rural country areas. These priests represented the bishop to the community and would celebrate the Eucharist on Sunday. The bishop would show unity with the priests in the outlying areas by sending the *fermentum* or a part of the eucharistic bread that he had consecrated.

Today this particle of the host no longer comes to us from the bishop, nor from a previous Mass, yet the priest still adds a small piece of the consecrated host to the cup. It is no longer called the *fermentum*, but "comingling," and primarily symbolizes the unity of the Body and Blood of Christ, as well as the unity of our sharing in the Body of Christ at Mass.

KNEELING

The *GIRM* states, "In the Dioceses of the United States of America, [the faithful] should kneel beginning after the singing or recitation of the *Sanctus* (Holy, Holy, Holy) until after the Amen of the Eucharistic Prayer, except when prevented on occasion by ill health, or for reasons of lack of space, of the large number of people present, or for another reasonable cause....The faithful kneel after the *Agnus Dei* (Lamb of God) unless the Diocesan Bishop determines otherwise"

(*GIRM* 43). In short, Catholics in the United States are asked to kneel during the Eucharistic Prayer.

The early Christians more than likely did not kneel but stood with the risen Christ as they prayed to God. Kneeling made its way into the liturgy both as a penitential posture and as a sign of reverence. Twenty-first-century Catholics kneel during Lent as a sign of penance and during the Eucharistic Prayer as a sign of reverence in the presence of the Blessed Sacrament.

In addition to our common liturgical posture of kneeling, many people find that kneeling during private prayer helps their prayer and deepens their spirituality.

BEING SILENT

It is hard to find silence when our culture surrounds us with sound, aside from journeying to an abbey tucked away in a forest or trekking to a mountaintop. We are immersed in so much sound from morning until evening, it can cause us to wonder what kind of emptiness we are trying to fill with this sound. Because of this, it is not surprising that people are uncomfortable with silence when they come to celebrate the liturgy. Nevertheless, the Church asks us to observe silence at certain times during the celebration of the Eucharist.

During each of these moments, it becomes clear that silence is not just an absence of sound. Rather, silence is observed to offer space that invites us to open our hearts to something or someone else. We observe silence at the time of the penitential rite so we can think about our lives and whether we have lived our baptismal calling in word and deed. Every time the priest says, "Let us pray," we are invited to offer our own silent prayers that he then "collects" in a spoken prayer. After some silence, the priest gathers all our individual prayers into one prayer and prays aloud. After the proclamation of the Scripture readings, some silence is observed so we can meditate on the meaning of the readings in our lives. We do the same at the conclusion of the homily. Finally, after receiving Communion, we pause in silence to give thanks and praise for the magnificent deeds God has accomplished for us in Jesus Christ.

Experiencing silence during the liturgy also serves as a model for our own lives and the good it can be for our spiritual health. Small moments of silence experienced during the course of the day—at the beginning, or at the end of the day—offer an opportunity to pray and ponder how God is present in our lives. Silence can also teach us to listen to God's guidance.

PLACING OF ASHES

The custom of imposing ashes on Ash Wednesday has biblical and liturgical roots. Both the Old Testament and the New Testament tell of those who wore repentant sackcloth and dusted themselves with ashes. The Book of Esther tells the story of how Mordecai mourned when he learned of the plot to kill all of the Jews. "When Mordecai learned all that had been done, Mordecai tore his clothes and put on sackcloth and ashes, and went through the city, wailing with a loud and bitter cry; he went up to the entrance of the king's gate, for no one might enter the king's gate clothed with sackcloth. In every province, wherever the king's command and his decree came, there was great mourning among the Jews, with fasting and weeping and lamenting, and most of them lay in sackcloth and ashes" (Esther 4:1–3).

Job, too, used ashes as a sign of repentance: "Therefore I despise myself, and repent in dust and ashes" (Job 42:6). Even the New Tes-

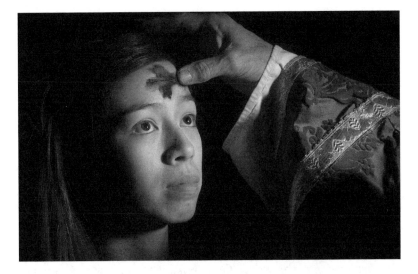

tament speaks about ashes as a sign of repentance. "Then he began to reproach the cities in which most of his deeds of power had been done, because they did not repent. 'Woe to you, Chorazin! Woe to you, Bethsaida! For if the deeds of power done in you had been done in Tyre and Sidon, they would have repented long ago in sackcloth and ashes'" (Matthew 11:20–21).

The liturgical custom of sprinkling ashes is undoubtedly inspired by the biblical use, and it probably originated in the Order of Penitents, a group of people established during the fourth century that consisted of those Christians who had committed grave sins and were admitted into the order by the bishop. The Order of Penitents predates the sacrament of reconciliation and was the only recourse that Christians had to regain salvation after they broke their baptismal promises. The imposition of ashes by the bishop was part of the rite for admittance into the Order of Penitents, and it is thought that at some point family members joined the penitents in receiving ashes. Eventually, recognizing that all human persons are sinners in need of repentance, all Christians began to present themselves for the imposition of ashes on Ash Wednesday, the day on which the penitents began their journey toward repentance.

The earliest mention of the existence of Ash Wednesday, known as *Dies Cinerum* or "the Day of Ashes," dates to the tenth century. However, it is believed that the custom for all Christians to receive ashes on Ash Wednesday was observed as early as the eighth century.

The imposition of ashes has always held a penitential character and continues to this day. With this public act of penitence, Catholics indicate that we are in need of forgiveness and that forty days of fasting, prayer, and almsgiving in preparation of the celebration of the Easter Triduum have begun.

The ashes used in the liturgy of Ash Wednesday come from the palms that were used during the previous year's celebration of Palm Sunday of our Lord's passion. Ashes are usually placed on the forehead in the shape of the cross, although in some communities they are more generously strewn over the crown of the penitent's head. The minister uses the words God spoke when expelling Adam and Eve from paradise, thus subjecting them to death, when imposing the ashes, "[Remember that] 'you are dust, and to dust you shall return'" (Genesis 3:19). Or, "Repent, and believe in the Gospel."

FAITHFUL REFLECTIONS

Visitors at a Catholic liturgy are sometimes amazed at all of the postures that are part of our prayer. Our ritual invites us to be present not just with our minds but with our bodies as we process, genuflect, kneel, sit, stand, bow, prostrate. More amazing is that at times we might do these gestures automatically, without realizing what they mean or knowing why we do them. When we slow down, we might realize we don't think about them much at all. Take some time to meditate on one or two of these gestures at some point during a day or the next time you go to Mass. Think about how your body feels as you kneel and pray or when you bow to the altar, as if Christ were standing there in front of you. In fact, that is what we are doing. Sometimes we don't know what to say when we come to prayer, yet one gesture can say it all. What would it be like to pray without words and let our bodies do the talking?

+ *What actions in your life do you do without thinking? What do you do by routine?*

+ *Make a point to really think about what you are doing when you sign yourself with the sign of the cross. What would it be like to bless a family member or friend with the sign of the cross?*

+ *How do you experience liturgical gestures outside of Mass? What is the difference between standing in line at Communion and standing in line at the grocery store? What other liturgical gestures might offer an opportunity for reflection beyond the church doors?*

CHAPTER NINE

SENSES AND SEASONAL DÉCOR

L iturgical décor is an intrinsic part of the celebration of the liturgy. It helps to engage all the senses in order to enhance the liturgical experience of everyone who participates in it. The power of the senses can take us into another world, beyond our knowing, as I learned when I traveled to Iceland in order to witness the midnight sun.

I had never been to Iceland, and I was looking forward to experiencing not only the midnight sun but to find out more about the mythic gnomes, elves, giants, and "hidden people" for which Iceland is known. From the moment we landed, I was enchanted. Iceland is ninety-nine percent volcanic desert, so arriving there is almost like landing on the moon, or so I imagined.

Passing of the cross during Tenebrae on Good Friday, The Basilica of Saint Mary, Minneapolis

As I marveled at the landscape on our way to Reykjavik, the capital of Iceland, the cab driver stopped unexpectedly and told us to get out and have a look at the geysers and shacks in the distance. Abandoning our suitcases in the cab, my traveling companion and I hiked through a volcanic landscape dotted by geysers to a vast collection of strange shacks where we discovered fish heads hanging on strings drying in the wind and the sun. The combination of the smell of sulfur produced by the geyser and the smell of drying fish created an olfactory experience that is not easily forgotten.

We continued on to Reykjavik, and after dinner set out for a walk through the city. As anticipated, the sun did not set but dipped to the horizon and back up. This movement created elongated shadows in the city that, accompanied by fog, set the stage for the folklore of elves and giants to come to life.

While admiring the Lutheran cathedral that is intriguingly shaped like a geyser, I realized we were surrounded by the eerily lifelike-looking statues of gnomes and elves that seemed to rise from low wafts of fog. It all was a bit unsettling, then all of a sudden an old woman appeared out of nowhere, as if she were one of the sculptures come to life. She motioned for us to join her and asked if we had heard that the night belongs to the gnomes. We told her we had not. Then she shrieked that the gnomes would kill us and we would not see the sun rise to its zenith, as she swung her scarf around my neck to pull me closer to her. In complete and absolute fear, I pushed her away and ran back to the safety of my locked hotel. Although I knew that gnomes and giants did not exist, my senses, the fog, the twisted geysers, smells of sulfur, and the cackle of the old woman all—but for the briefest of moments—led me to imagine that we would be killed by gnomes and not leave the island alive.

Against all logic, our senses picked up explicit and implicit messages that amplified the prophetic words of the old woman. This is how décor supports the liturgy as it engages the senses through smells and bells and festive or solemn décor to better communicate its message of faith. How often have I heard people say, "It smells like Christmas," when they enter a church filled with evergreens? Or, "It smells like

Easter," when they approach a baptismal font surrounded by Easter lilies? Throughout the course of the liturgical year, the décor changes to support and enhance the meaning of the seasons and feasts. Some seasons are marked by a more modest décor, while others are exuberant and filled with abundant symbols as we remember the fullness of Christ's life, death, and resurrection.

SEASONAL SYMBOLS FOR THE INCARNATION CYCLE

The Incarnation season includes the liturgical seasons of Advent and Christmas. The word "Advent" originates from the Latin phrase *Adventus Domini*, "the arrival of the Lord." It refers to Jesus' appearance on earth more than 2,000 years ago, his presence with us today, and especially his coming at the end of time. Thus the season of Advent is filled with anticipation to commemorate the birth of Jesus and prepare for his final manifestation, the Second Coming. Christmas celebrates the fullness of these realities: Jesus' presence among us yesterday, today, and tomorrow.

Advent mobile by Lucinda Naylor

THE ADVENT WREATH

The origin of the Advent wreath is unclear. There is evidence of a pre-Christian custom of decorating a wheel with candles, while prayers were offered for the wheel of the earth to be turned so that light and warmth would return. Christians then adopted this ritual and began to use it in domestic settings during the Middle Ages. By the year 1500, more formal practices surrounding the Advent wreath had developed with the wreath symbolizing new and eternal life gained through the life, death, and resurrection of Jesus Christ.

The circular shape of the Advent wreath has neither beginning nor end and signifies eternal life. The evergreens, too, represent eternal life, with holly implying immortality, cedar expressing strength and healing, laurel touting victory over suffering, and pinecones and nuts lauding life and resurrection. The four candles that were added to the wreath over time represent the four weeks of Advent. According to some traditions, these candles are purple, connecting them to the color for the Advent season. Sometimes the color of the candle for the third Sunday of Advent is rose like the vestments for that day. This color celebrates the fact that we have reached the midpoint of Advent. The Latin name for this day is not surprisingly *Gaudete*, which means "rejoice." Today the Advent wreath is the central symbol of the Advent season in most churches. The candles are sometimes purple and rose, or they may be white. Today's liturgy includes a blessing of the wreath and candlelighting on the first Sunday of Advent.

Since the use of the Advent wreath originated in the homes of Christians, families are often invited to continue this custom. Advent wreaths can be easily constructed, and the candle of each week lit and blessed as part of a meal prayer on the Saturdays or Sundays of Advent. Prayers for these blessings can be found in the *Catholic Book of Blessings*.

THE CHRISTMAS TREE

The earliest reports of decorated trees date back to ancient Roman times, when small trees were decorated with pieces of polished metal during the winter festival of Saturnalia to honor Saturn, the god of agriculture. During the Middle Ages, Adam and Eve were commemorated with mystical plays on Christmas Eve, and an evergreen was decorated with apples to symbolize the tree of paradise. Some people believe Martin Luther was the first to introduce a tree decorated with candles into the home when he was inspired by the star-filled

sky he encountered during a walk through the woods on a clear Christmas night.

By the nineteenth century, however, the custom of Christians decorating a tree in their homes had become popular in the Western Hemisphere. Today more than thirty-five million Christmas trees are sold in the United States a year for use in homes, public places, and as part of the Christmas décor in our churches.

Whether it is placed outside or inside the church, a Christmas tree is a wonderful symbol of the tree of life, the tree of paradise. It brings joy to people's hearts as they indulge in feelings of nostalgia from childhood memories and invites people to look toward the future when the promise of eternal life will be fulfilled. Christmas trees offer not only a visual enhancement to the liturgical décor, but one of smell that immediately greets all who come to worship and signals that Christmas has arrived. The church not only looks like Christmas, but it smells like Christmas.

THE MANGER

Saint Francis is often credited with the popularization of the Christmas manger. However, this custom predates his life as a saint, since he lived during the twelfth century. Already by the fifth century, the Basilica of Saint Mary Major in Rome featured a chapel with a representation of the scene of Jesus' birth as described in the Gospels and visualized by artists.

Although Saint Francis did not invent the use of the manger, he certainly gave it a deeper theological interpretation, as the Child in the crib allowed him to meditate on the mystery of God becoming human. In addition to the Baby, Francis also had great devotion to the suffering Jesus on the cross, and both became important to the spirituality of people across Europe.

After Francis' death, crib-making became widespread throughout Europe and eventually throughout the world. Today Christmas scenes known as mangers or crèches are displayed in almost every church at Christmas, as well as in family homes where the cultural and ethnic marks of many different peoples are able to be expressed. The setting-up of the manger has also become part of many Advent celebrations and moves into Christmas when the Baby Jesus is ceremoniously placed in the manger, accompanied by the singing of Christmas songs and carols. It can also be incorporated with an entrance procession continuing to the crib, where a prayer and a blessing might be prayed.

SEASONAL SYMBOLS FOR THE PASCHAL CYCLE

The paschal cycle lasts ninety days and celebrates the core of the Christian faith: the life, death, and resurrection of Jesus Christ. The three-day-celebration of the Easter Triduum forms the center of the paschal cycle. This Christian Passover commences after sunset on Holy Thursday and concludes at sunset on Easter Sunday. The Easter Triduum is preceded by a forty-day Lenten period of preparation that runs from Ash Wednesday to Holy Thursday, then opens out to fifty days of joy, symbolic of the new age of resurrection, and concludes with Pentecost Sunday, the fiftieth and last day of the Easter season. Décor for the paschal season progresses from Ash Wednesday, through Lent, and into the Easter season to culminate in the Feast of Pentecost.

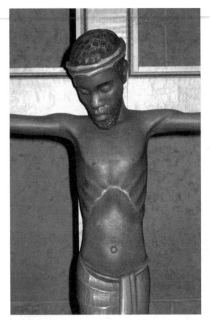

African crucifix

LENTEN SIMPLICITY

The season of Lent is characterized by two major sacramental themes, baptism and penance. Catechumens—who will enter the Church through the sacraments of initiation (baptism, confirmation, and Eucharist)—complete their preparation, baptized Christians prepare to reconcile with the Church through the sacrament of reconciliation, and the entire Christian community engages in the Lenten disciplines of prayer, fasting, and almsgiving.

The décor for Lent is marked by a sparseness that reflects the penitential character of the season. Therefore, Lenten décor relies on taking away rather than adding to the visual environment. Lenten décor is marked by visual absence, rather than visual excess, and echoes the call of the season to clear our lives of clutter and return to the essentials of our faith.

VEILING OF CROSSES AND CRUCIFIXES

Some churches have the custom of covering crucifixes during Lent or of emptying the baptismal font. In both

South American crucifix

instances, thoughtful reflection is advised. Before the Second Vatican Council, it was customary to veil crucifixes and statues beginning on the fourth Sunday of Lent. This Sunday is also known as *Laetare* Sunday, which is Latin for "rejoice," because it marks the halfway point of Lent. Crucifixes were then unveiled after the Good Friday service, and statues were unveiled at the beginning of the Easter Vigil.

The revision of the liturgy after Vatican II left the decision to continue this practice to the vote of individual conferences of bishops. The United States Conference of Catholic Bishops never voted on this matter, so it was not allowed in the United States. With the third edition of *The Roman Missal*, the U.S. Conference of Catholic Bishops reviewed the matter again and voted to allow the covering of crosses from the conclusion of the Mass on Saturday of the fourth week of Lent until the end of the celebration of the Lord's passion on Good Friday. In addition, they voted to allow sacred images to be covered from the conclusion of the Mass on Saturday of the fourth week of Lent until the beginning of the Easter Vigil. In both instances, the covering is allowed but not required.

While it is true that the Church has a long tradition of fasting from images and colors during Lent, the medieval paintings on high altars often had side panels that could be closed during Lent. The inside painting was always colorful, while the outside panels were painted in gray tones. During penitential seasons the panels were closed so people would fast from colors yet be encouraged in their Lenten disciplines by the saints and saintly motives painted on the outside panels. Although we fast from colors during penitential seasons, we do not fast from all that the saints have to teach us. On the contrary, we are to focus on the lives of the saints so we may be inspired to become better Christians. The same holds for the cross. Seeing and meditating on the crucified Christ probably enhances our devotion more than gazing upon a cloth covering it.

EMPTY FONTS AND FOUNTS

Some churches maintain a custom of emptying baptismal fonts and holy water containers during Lent. Some even go so far as to fill them with desert metaphors, such as sand and cacti. Although this sort of décor is well-intentioned, it does not raise up the primary focus of the season, which is those preparing for baptism at the Easter Vigil. Nor is it clear how this practice engenders a greater commitment on the part of those who are preparing to renew their baptismal vows. There is, however, an ancient custom of emptying the baptismal font after the Mass of the Lord's Supper on Holy Thursday and leaving it empty on Good Friday. This emptiness emphasizes the anticipation we have for the new baptismal water that will be blessed during the Easter Vigil.

The washing of the feet

DÉCOR FOR THE EASTER TRIDUUM

The décor for celebrating the liturgies of the Triduum comprises the symbols that are used for the liturgies themselves. There is little need to add additional décor, since the liturgy itself provides such rich imagery with its symbols for each of the days.

On Holy Thursday, we wash feet, we process with the gifts for the poor, we carry the Blessed Sacrament, and we strip the altar. On Good Friday, the tabernacle is emptied and we unveil and kiss the wood of the cross. On Holy Saturday, we gather around the Easter fire, we light the paschal candle and our individual tapers, then we process into a darkened church to bless water, dunk the Easter candle into its waters, immerse the elect into the font, and anoint them with sacred chrism, as they, dripping with the waters of new life, dress in white to reenter the church and join the offertory procession as gifts from and to our community. Given the number and complexity of the symbols and images that are used during the Triduum, additional décor would detract from, rather than enhance, the liturgy during these days.

The veneration of the cross

EASTER LILIES

Although the rich symbolism of the Easter Vigil and the celebration of Easter are far more important than anything else we could add to the décor, there are some things the faithful have come to expect, such as Easter lilies. These flowers have come to symbolize the resurrection by both sight and scent. Spring flowers often continue this generative visual expression of new life throughout the Easter season.

RED FOR PENTECOST

The decorative strength of the Feast of Pentecost lies in its color. Since this day celebrates the descent of the Holy Spirit on the apostles in the form of flames, the Church chose red as the color of the day. Most church buildings look great when decked out in red. In addition to red vestments, red paraments, or ornamental hangings, such as a cover for the ambo and an *antependium* or a hanging for the altar are often used. Red processional banners can also enhance the processions and celebration, as do any red flowers.

Parishioners can also be invited to wear red that day, since they are the Church gathered and equally deserving of adornment. It is a beautiful and moving sight to see both the church building and the Church dressed in red.

FAITHFUL REFLECTIONS

Liturgical décor is a part of the liturgy that lends itself to both creativity and the crossing of borders. What would the liturgical year look like in your home? The colors of the liturgical year offer the opportunity to expand décor and seasonality into our homes, offices, wardrobe, and even food. Preparing for each liturgical season can become part of your prayer as an individual, couple, or family as you meditate reflectively while preparing a seasonal meal or your home décor. Reflect a little bit each day during the Incarnation or paschal seasons.

✦ *What sights and smells of the church touch your soul the most? Why?*

✦ *What are the strongest symbols that are part of the liturgical décor in your parish? What makes them meaningful for you?*

✦ *What can you do to make each of these seasons more meaningful for you or your family?*

CHAPTER TEN

MONOGRAMS, ACRONYMS, AND IMAGES

We are surrounded by sacred images every day. They range from religious bumper stickers on cars, to billboards lining the highway, necklaces, earrings, and even logo branding on some products in the grocery store. Sometimes these images are borrowed from other religions, but most often they are Christian images. Some are quite obvious, such as a cross or a crucifix. Others are more complex, such as a fish or a pelican or even a reversed fish with tiny legs. Still others are nearly incomprehensible because they are acronyms based on a Greek or Latin phrase.

Many statues of the lives of those who have witnessed their faith also surround us. Statuary is most often found in churches or chapels, but sometimes they have a special place

Saint Michael atop a streetlight, Ghent, Belgium

in our homes or in small prayer gardens. Many saints are well-known and easily recognizable, such as the Blessed Mother, who appeared in Mexico as Our Lady of Guadalupe. Others are not as familiar, as when Our Lady of La'Vang, presented herself as the Mother of God amid the healing La'Vang fern plant in Vietnam in the eighteenth century. Our Lady of La'Vang consoled the persecuted Vietnamese Christians and was present to them as they prepared to die because of their commitment to Christianity.

There are also unfamiliar faith images connected with familiar saints. Most of us might be able to identify Saint Joseph or the Sacred Heart of Jesus, but we may not know why Saint Joseph holds a lily and where the image of the Sacred Heart originated. Other images are even more confusing, such as a man carrying a baby on his shoulders, as is the case with Saint Christopher, or a woman holding what looks like eyeballs on a platter, as is the case with Saint Lucy.

In order to understand some of these images, it is helpful to know about the sacred monograms, acronyms, and images that can help unlock the secrets that are part of many statues found in our churches.

SACRED MONOGRAMS

Monograms and acronyms were used to communicate, in a semihidden way, that a certain home belonged to a Christian family or that a certain tomb held the body of a Christian. This was especially important during times of persecution. Monograms combine two or more letters and overlap them to form one symbol. Acronyms are a series of initials that only those who had been initiated into the faith were able to read. This allowed the baptized—and only them—to know that they were in a Christian home or near a Christian tomb.

Today we see monograms and acronyms throughout our churches, but we are often unaware of their meaning or their origin. If you look closely, you might find them carved in altars, painted on church walls, or embroidered on vestments. What do they mean and why are they there?

Mosaic of Jesus Christ, Hagia Sophia, Istanbul, Turkey

Many monograms focus on Christ and consist of a combination of letters that refer to the name of Jesus Christ. The most common and most ancient of all Christ monograms is the combination of the Greek letters Chi **X** and Rho **P**. These are often superimposed with the **X** placed slightly beneath the **P**. They are the first two letters of the Greek name for Christ, *Kristos*.

Another Christ monogram consists of three letters that are always capitalized, **IHS**. These are the first two and the last letter of the Greek name of Jesus, which have been transliterated using the Latin alphabet. Another form of this monogram used during the Middle Ages was **IHC**. In this case the letter Sigma, the last letter of the Greek name of Jesus, is transliterated into a **C**, rather than an **S**. Another form is when the **I** is replaced with a **J**. Both **I** and **J** and **C** and **S** were used interchangeably in the Latin alphabet until around the eighteenth century. In keeping with this pattern of transliteration, you might see **IHS, IHC, JHS** or **JHC**. All four of these have the same meaning. They are a monogram, or a concealed way to express the word "Jesus."

Another version of the Christ monogram is **ICXC**. This includes the first and last transliterated letters of the Greek version of Jesus (**IC**) and Christ (**XC**). Painted icons often contain these letters, but they are split on either side of the icon image, with **IC** for Jesus on the left and **XC** for Christ on the right.

These monograms are constant invitations to honor the name of Jesus, at least for those who can read them. While it was necessary to conceal their meaning when they were created, it is now more helpful for us to understand them in order to fully receive their message when placed in the larger context of church interiors and statuary.

SACRED ACRONYMS

In addition to monograms, churches house another combination of letters, known as acronyms, an example of which is the often-seen **INRI**. Most crucifixes have these letters carved in the wood above the head of Jesus or written on a small plaque nailed to the cross. This acronym stands for the Latin sentence *Iesus Christus, Rex Iudeorum,* or in English, "Jesus Christ, King of the Jews." The text is taken directly from the Gospel of John, "Pilate also had an inscription written and put on the cross. It read, 'Jesus of Nazareth, the King of the Jews.' Many of the Jews read this inscription, because the place where Jesus was crucified was near the city; and it was written in Hebrew, in Latin, and in Greek" (John 19:19–20).

It is believed that when Saint Helena, the mother of Emperor Con-

stantine, traveled to the Holy Land, she not only recovered parts of the cross on which Jesus was crucified, but that, in 325, she also found the shroud in which the body of Jesus had been wrapped and the tablet, with this inscription, placed on the cross by Pilate. The tablet is known as the *Titulus Crucis.* It was brought to Rome by Pope Gregory the Great at the end

Above: Superimposed A(ve) M(aria)

of the fifth century and has been preserved in the church of *Santa Croce* (Holy Cross) in Rome since 1124.

Another popular combination of letters is **AΩ**, the Greek letters alpha and omega. These are the first and last letters of the Greek alphabet and refer to Christ as expressed in the Book of Revelation, "'I am the Alpha and the Omega', says the Lord God, who is and who was and who is to come, the Almighty" (Revelation 1:8). These words have been ascribed to Jesus Christ. Thus the **AΩ** are a reference to him.

In addition to the many Christ-centered acronyms, there is another that is a popular decorative element in our churches and refers to Mary. It is a combination of the letters **A** and **M**, either next to one another or laid over each other. They are the first letters spoken to Mary by the archangel Gabriel greeting Mary at the time of the annunciation. These first words were *Ave Maria*, meaning "hail" or "hello," Mary. They are also the first words of the popular prayer to Mary, known by that same name, Hail Mary.

Like the Christ monograms, acronym letter combinations are constant invitations to prayer, even if they are short prayers, such as the Hail Mary. Every time we see **INRI**, it is a reminder of the sacrifice of Christ. Every time we see **AΩ**, it is a reminder of who Christ really is, the beginning and the end of all that is. When we see **AM**, it is a reminder of the role Mary played in the mystery of our salvation as the Mother of Christ. In all three instances, the acronyms call us to prayer.

SACRED IMAGES

Our churches and other sacred places like the catacombs contain sacred images that, like acronyms and monograms, do not always make sense upon first glance. We might be puzzled as to why the priest is wearing a cope with birds all over it. What is the meaning of the fish that is carved into the walls of the catacombs and found all over on key chains, T-shirts, and car bumpers? It apparently is Christian, but where does it come from, and what does it mean?

FISH

The image of a fish is an ancient Christian symbol. Like monograms and acronyms, the fish was introduced as a sort of "secret code" image to allude to Christianity.

The fish symbol was used because the word for fish in Greek is *ichthys*. *Ichthys* also happens to be an acrostic or puzzle for the Greek *Iesos Christos Huios Theou, Soter,* which means "Jesus Christ Son of God, Savior." The first letter of each word of the Greek version of this Christological title spells out *ichthys*, or fish.

As with so many symbols, once they are created, theological minds and other inquiring minds attach additional meaning to them. An obvious connection may be found in the baptismal theology of Tertullian, who refers to Christ as the big fish and all Christians as little fish. This expressive statement led to the combination of small fish and one large fish in decorative motifs in baptismal architecture.

Tertullian's writing and other theological interpretations, such as linking the fish to the miraculous multiplication of the loaves and fish, added to the richness of the symbol. The Christian fish symbol has become so well-known that Darwinists, who study evolution, have adopted it as their own—with some changes that mock Christianity to make their point. The Darwinists' fish symbol is turned around to the left, little feet are added, and *Darwin* is written inside the outline of the fish. Indeed, symbols have the power to communicate many meanings, so much so that they are sometimes co-opted to diminish their impact.

THE PELICAN

A popular medieval symbol for Christ is the mother pelican surrounded by her chicks. In most of these images, the mother pelican is shown to be picking her chest and allowing her chicks to feed on her blood. This is based on the medieval belief that pelican mothers fed their chicks their own blood when they had no other food to give them, even if it meant that the pelican mother might die.

The Christian connection is rather clear: The mother pelican gave her life to save her chicks like Jesus gave his

Tabernacle with mother pelican and her chicks

life so we might live. However, if we do not know the story of the pelican, it is easy to miss the power of this symbol.

The pelican image is most often seen on altars, tabernacles, ceilings of eucharistic chapels, vestments, and altar hangings. Its image is also present in the hymn *Adoro te Devote,* composed by Saint Thomas Aquinas for the feast of *Corpus Christi*, the Body and Blood of Christ. The second-to-the-last verse reads in free translation, "Lord Jesus, Pelican of Mercy, with your precious blood, cleanse me from my sins." What a sacred link between sacrament and nature.

TETRAMORPH

"Tetramorph" comes from the Greek words *tetra*, meaning "four," and *morph*, meaning "shape." Tetramorph thus refers to a combination of four different shapes that together make a whole. In Christianity, this term is used to refer to the symbolic representation of the four evangelists, Matthew, Mark, Luke, and John, who wrote the accounts of the life of Jesus. The different shapes attributed to each apostle are based on the description of the four living creatures in the Book of the prophet Ezekiel and in the Book of Revelation.

"As I looked, a stormy wind came out of the north: a great cloud with brightness around it and fire flashing forth continually, and in the middle of the fire, something like gleaming amber. In the middle of it was something like four living creatures. This was their appearance: they were of human form. Each had four faces, and each of them had four wings. Their legs were straight, and the soles of their feet were like the sole of a calf's foot; and they sparkled like burnished bronze. Under their wings on their four sides they had human hands. And the four had their faces and their wings thus: their wings touched one another; each of them moved straight ahead, without turning as they moved. As for

the appearance of their faces: the four had the face of a human being, the face of a lion on the right side, the face of an ox on the left side, and the face of an eagle" (Ezekiel 1:4–10).

"In front of the throne there is something like a sea of glass, like crystal. Around the throne, and on each side of the throne, are four living creatures, full of eyes in front and behind: the first living creature like a lion, the second living creature like an ox, the third living creature with a face like a human face, and the fourth living creature like a flying eagle" (Revelation 4:6–7).

Based on these texts, artists began to depict the four evangelists as the four living creatures surrounding the throne on which Christ is seated.

In some cases, the evangelist is depicted in the form of the symbol that represents him, such as Saint John being shown as an eagle or Luke as a winged ox. Sometimes they are represented in human form, with an image of their living creature next to them. Thus, Saint Mark might be shown writing his Gospel with a lion sitting at his side, or Matthew with an angel next to him. Matthew is connected with an angel or winged man, Luke with an ox, Mark with a lion, and John with an eagle.

A popular place for the Tetramorph to be located is near the ambo or the place from where the Gospel is proclaimed. Sometimes the *Gospel Book* itself is decorated with a Tetramorph. In both instances, the connection between the Gospel and the Gospel writers is obvious because of the association of the Tetramorph images. Altars and baptismal fonts have also been decorated with the Tetramorph because it is in baptism that we are baptized into the life, death, and resurrection of Jesus as proclaimed by the evangelists. Baptism is also our entrance to the Eucharist, where we celebrate the life, death, and resurrection of Jesus as narrated in the Gospels.

*Tetramorph carving decorating the altar at
Shrine of the Little Flower, Albuquerque*

SAINTS AND THEIR ATTRIBUTES

In the same way that the evangelists are depicted with their symbols based on one of four living creatures, most saints are represented with a symbol that allows us to identify the specific saint. For example, we might see Saint Peter holding a key, signifying that Jesus gave him the keys to the kingdom, or Saint Clare holding a monstrance, which is reminiscent of when she defended her monastery while holding a monstrance that warded off the enemy. It is helpful to know a bit about the lives of the saints so that their identities are more easily recognized.

THE SACRED HEART OF JESUS

The Sacred Heart of Jesus is a very popular statue that can be found in most churches and in many homes. Although devotion to the love of Christ existed from the early days of the Church, specific devotions to the Sacred Heart of Jesus did not exist until about the tenth century and were mostly private. Public devotions to the Sacred Heart of Jesus evolved in response to the visions of Sister Mary Margaret Alacoque, a Visitation sister who lived in the seventeenth century. In her visions, Jesus spoke of his love for the people and his disappointment about the lack of love that he saw reciprocated toward him. He called for a feast that would celebrate his love and repair the lack of love he saw demonstrated. As a result of Sister Mary Margaret's visions, the Feast of the Sacred Heart of

Jesus was founded and is still celebrated today on the Friday after the solemnity of the Body and Blood of Christ.

The image of the Sacred Heart shows Jesus presenting his heart to us. It is a heart on fire with love for people. It is topped with a crown of thorns that reminds us of Jesus' sacrificial love and the fact that he loves us so much that he was willing to die for us. This statue expresses Jesus' love for us, calls us to a profound sense of gratitude, and invites us to share in his same sacrificial love for God's people. Like Jesus, we are asked to love without condition, even if that means giving our very life for our neighbor.

THE BLESSED VIRGIN MARY

Representations of Mary, the Mother of Jesus, are found in most every cathedral, church, or chapel. Statues of Mary have been created in wood, bronze, stone, and plaster. Her image is embroidered on banners, tapestries, and chasubles, as well as portrayed in paintings, frescos, stained-glass windows, and mosaics. Images of Mary are also found in relation to the many different visions or theological understandings of her role in the history of salvation. Some of the more common representations are Our Lady of the Immaculate Conception, Our Lady of Czestochowa, and Our Lady of Guadalupe. They are but a small representation of the many ways that our blessed Mother is able to show her infinite care for humanity as the Mother of our Lord.

Our Lady of Sorrows
by Mary Romero Cash

OUR LADY OF THE IMMACULATE CONCEPTION

Our Lady of the Immaculate Conception is probably one of the most widespread images of Mary. The doctrine of the Immaculate Conception that tells us Mary was born without personal or original sin, coming from the word *macula* in Latin, was pronounced in 1854. The devotion and depictions of the Immaculate Conception, though, predate this dogma by several centuries.

Details of this depiction may differ from image to image, but most renditions of the Immaculate Conception show Mary standing on the moon and crowned with twelve stars, as referenced in the Book of Revelation: "A great portent appeared in heaven: a woman clothed with the sun, with the moon under her feet, and on her head a crown of twelve stars" (Revelation 12:1).

A popular addition to the imagery is the serpent trampled by Mary's foot that refers to the original sin that came into the world through the cunning of the snake and the disobedience of Adam and Eve. Mary, as the new Eve, crushes the snake because she will give birth to the Savior who will reopen the gates to heaven that had been closed to all.

In 1847, Our Lady of the Immaculate Conception was declared the Patron Saint of the United States of America. Devotion increased substantially in 1858, after the apparition of Mary to Bernadette Soubirous, a young girl in France, where Bernadette quoted Mary as saying, "I am the Immaculate Conception." This encounter led to the famous Our Lady of Lourdes Grotto and many miraculous healings associated with prayer to Our Lady of the Immaculate Conception. Her feast is celebrated on December 8 and is a holy day of obligation in the United States.

OUR LADY OF CZESTOCHOWA

The image of our Lady of Czestochowa holding the baby Jesus is recognizable by the fact that their faces are black and there is a double scar on Mary's right cheek. She is also known as the Black Madonna of Czestochowa.

The history of this icon is complex and wrapped in mystery. Some people say it was painted by Saint Luke and handed down through history. What is certain is that this icon has been in Czestochowa, Poland, since 1381.

The black color is the result of a fire that occurred in the church. Our Lady of Czestochowa is credited with having saved the church from complete destruction. The scars on her face are said to have been inflicted on the image when the church was robbed by thieves. It is said that when the looters tried to flee with the church's treasures, their horses refused to move. In anger, they threw the image of our Lady onto the floor and stabbed her several times. Some versions of the story say the image started to bleed. Others say the robber who inflicted the wounds fell to the ground and died when he attempted a third slash. Early attempts to restore the painting failed, and even today the faces are blackened and the scars are present.

Our Lady of Czestochowa was declared the queen and protector of Poland in 1656. Today her shrine remains the most popular shrine in Poland. She is also revered by people of Polish descent throughout the world.

OUR LADY OF GUADALUPE

Throughout Christian history, Mary has appeared in almost every part of the world to encourage people, give them hope, or call them to more holy lives. In nearly every one of those instances, she has presented herself in the image of the people to whom she appeared.

The most well-known apparition in the Americas is Our Lady of Guadalupe. She appeared as an Aztec princess to Juan Diego, a local Mexican peasant, in 1531. When his bishop asked for proof of her appearance, our Lady showed Juan Diego a rosebush that was blooming in winter. She told him to wrap the red roses in his mantle or poncho and bring them to the bishop. When he opened his mantle to show the roses to the bishop, an exact image of the beautiful Lady Juan Diego had seen appeared on the mantle. This mantle is made from yucca fiber and is still preserved and on display, with the image intact, at the Basilica of Our Lady of Guadalupe in Mexico City.

Our Lady of Guadalupe is most often depicted with references to the Book of Revelation, Chapter 12. She is clad with the rays of the sun, standing on the moon, and her blue mantle is covered with stars.

Today many churches host an image or a shrine of Our Lady of Guadalupe. Her feast is celebrated on December 12, and she was named the patroness of the Americas by Blessed Pope John Paul II in 1999.

SAINT JOSEPH

One of the most popular saints, next to the Blessed Mother, is Saint Joseph. He is usually depicted as holding a child with his left arm and a blooming staff of lilies in his right hand. The child depicted is Jesus, the foster child of Saint Joseph. The meaning of the lily is a bit more complicated. One explanation is that the lily is a symbol of chastity, since we praise Joseph as the most-chaste spouse of Mary, the Mother of Jesus. This particular interpretation of the lily comes later than the initial origin of the flowers that is based on an ancient story about the selection of Joseph as the husband of Mary. According to the story, Joseph, like all men who were eligible for marriage at that time, was given a walking staff. When it was given to the others, nothing happened. However, when it was given to Joseph, the staff started to bloom and brought forth the lily. The elders saw this as a sign from God that Joseph was the chosen one. Thus the flower symbolizes the fact that God chose Joseph to be the father of Jesus on earth.

STATIONS OF THE CROSS

The celebration of the Stations of the Cross is one of the most popular devotional practices of the Catholic Church. Its concept as a spiritual journey through the last days of Jesus' life is rooted in a deep human need to see, touch, and experience places of personal, historic, or religious importance that were related to Jesus. Sometimes people will travel thousands of miles to remember and be present to a particular place or object that is full of meaning. Catholic football fans often travel across the country to visit the football stadium at Notre Dame and touch the statue of football coach Knute Rockne. Each year, millions of Catholics go to Rome to visit the tomb of the early martyrs and to pray with the pope. Muslims, Jews, and Christians alike visit Jerusalem, a place that is held holy by all three of these major religions.

The desire to visit places of important events and memory, such as Jerusalem, is not new. During the Middle Ages, Western European Christians not only visited the places where Jesus lived but also defended them from non-Christians. Thus some medieval Christians went to Jerusalem as pilgrims, while others traveled as crusaders. Regardless of their intent, those who returned to their homelands brought back stories and images of the holy sites.

A growing emphasis on our Lord's passion during a time in history that was plagued with disease, famine, and war—combined with these pilgrim stories—gave rise to the creation of shrines dedicated to the passion of our Lord. A devotion that followed the events of Jesus on his last journey, from his trial to his tomb, developed and was emphasized by the Franciscan friars through their preaching. Those who could not make the journey to the Holy Land participated in a mini-pilgrimage that was created close to home. Thus the Stations of the Cross was born.

Today's Stations of the Cross are portrayed as a meditation on Jesus' obedience unto death, God's unending love, and the frailty of our human condition.

The number of stations, as well as their emphasis, has changed over the centuries and continues to evolve. Today traditional stations have fourteen different moments of reflection. Some invite us to meditate on moments in Jesus' passion that are not found in Scripture but have been handed down to us by tradition, such as when Jesus

meets Veronica. A new version of this devotion now comprises fifteen stations that are all based in Scripture and end with the resurrection. On Good Friday in 1991, Blessed Pope John Paul II introduced this new set of fifteen stations during the annual stations held in the Roman Coliseum.

Top: Station VIII, Jesus meets the holy women, The Basilica of Saint Mary, Minneapolis

Left: Station VIII, Jesus meets the holy women, Cathedral of St. Vincent of Saragossa, Malo, France

Different churches display their stations in different ways. The most common presentation is for the images of the stations to be mounted on the outer perimeter walls of the church. This placement allows people to walk from one station to the next and experience the movement of a pilgrimage. Some churches have located their stations outside on church grounds. This allows for even more time and space to journey from one station to the next.

Although the stations can be celebrated on any day and at any time, community celebrations are often reserved for Fridays, the day that we commemorate the death of Jesus. This is especially appropriate and meaningful on Fridays during Lent and on Good Friday.

FAITHFUL REFLECTIONS

Our churches are filled with images that speak about our faith, serve as testimonies to our Christian history, and honor the saints who led the way with their faith, lives, and martyrdom. However, much of this witness is no longer recognized or understood because the meaning of imagery has been lost, forgotten, or distorted. Set aside some time to walk around your church and locate particular images that you might have walked by every day and not realized were there. Look to the altar for animal images that speak of sacrifice and Christ's selfless love. Look to the area of proclamation or the *Gospel Book* to find expressions of the holy apostles who recorded the testimonies of those who encountered Jesus' teaching and took on the task of passing them down to the generations that would follow after them. We each share that task and are called to pass on the stories of our faith by understanding and sharing the meaning of the symbols that are alive within the Mass and beyond. Knowledge of our faith is a wonderful gift. How will you pass on your gift to others?

✦ *Discover the monograms or acronyms present in your church. Learn why they are located where they are and share their meaning with someone.*

✦ *Identify the statues of saints in your church that you do not already know. Find their visual attribute, such as Saint Joseph's lily, and research what it means. Read about their lives and name one way you can learn and grow from their witness.*

✦ *Reflect on what Christian symbol is most powerful for you. How can it support you on your journey of faith?*

Top: Station VIII, Jesus meets the holy women, Church of Saint Peter, Mendota, Minnesota
Bottom: The Stations of the Cross are placed in an ambulatory aisle around the assembly to allow for procession while praying the stations, Church of Saint Peter, Mendota, Minnesota

CONCLUSION

I marvel at my niece's and nephew's ability to memorize the lyrics of songs. They often have an electronic device of some kind plugged into their ears as they bob their head, sway, and mouth the lyrics to a song I cannot hear. I don't know the lyrics to many songs, but occasionally a psalm refrain from Mass will stick in my mind and I am not able to let go of it. Although it is sometimes annoying, I count my blessings, because the song is one of faith, with meaningful words that can become part of my unconscious prayer.

How much more profound this experience must be for monks and nuns who pray the psalms throughout each day. No doubt they lose focus at times, but the words go through their minds, touch their hearts—and in the end—shape their souls. More importantly, the psalms provide them with a vocabulary and images that allow them to make sense of their life's experience and even their simplest daily encounters.

Not long ago, I witnessed a bicyclist cut off by a careless bus driver. The words that flowed from the young man's lips were not kind. I wondered how a member of a religious community might have reacted in the same situation. Maybe she would have used more inspired language rising from a heart formed by the psalms, "The Lord is my shepherd, I shall not want."

Like language, we also have images and symbols that can assist us in our daily encounters with life, sometimes consciously, more often unconsciously. Imagine standing by the ocean at sunset, with the wind

The path leading to the cross in Saint John's Abbey Cemetery,
Collegeville, Minnesota

blowing through your hair and the sounds and smell of the ocean all around you. Imagine the marvelous array of colors as the sun begins its journey to the horizon. On the pier, a lone pelican rests after a successful hunt. She is beautifully perched on the post of the dock with her face turned to the sun. While a picturesque sight for those who love nature, those who know Christian symbology are reminded of the love of Christ and our calling to give our life's blood on behalf of others, as a pelican is said to do for her young, and as Christ did for us. In that moment of contemplation, we are invited to ponder our salvation and the call of Christ in our lives. Thus is the power of symbols that surround us.

The Church provides us with symbols to help us see God's presence, as everything that surrounds us holds an invitation to enter into conversation with the divine. The pelican reminds us of Christ, while stars become symbols of Mary, and clovers reflect the Holy Trinity. A new world is waiting for those who seek to understand the language of the symbols of our faith.

The process of learning the language and symbols of our faith begins when we are first dipped into waters of baptism and anointed with the chrism of salvation. It continues throughout our earthly pilgrimage until our bodies are sprinkled with holy water for the last time during the rites of Christian burial.

This journey that each of us is called to make is beautifully displayed in the symbolic layout of the cemetery at Saint John's Abbey in Collegeville, Minnesota. The graveyard is positioned between a lake at the bottom of a hill and a cross at the top, with the sky beyond. The long road leading up from the lake to the cross is lined by golden poplars and surrounded by graves. It is a magnificent testimony of our Christian pilgrimage that begins in the waters of baptism and ends at the cross, our pathway to eternal life.

This is the path we all walk together. May God's blessings be yours as you encounter the symbols of hope and love and faith that await and surround you each day. Amen.